Mach Learning

The Most Complete Guide for Beginners to Mastering Deep Learning, Artificial Intelligence and Data Science with Python. This Book Includes: Python Machine Learning and Data Science.

Andrew Park

© **Copyright 2020 - All rights reserved.**

The content contained within this book may not be reproduced, duplicated or transmitted without direct written permission from the author or the publisher.

Under no circumstances will any blame or legal responsibility be held against the publisher, or author, for any damages, reparation, or monetary loss due to the information contained within this book. Either directly or indirectly.

Legal Notice:

This book is copyright protected. This book is only for personal use. You cannot amend, distribute, sell, use, quote or paraphrase any part, or the content within this book, without the consent of the author or publisher.

Disclaimer Notice:

Please note the information contained within this document is for educational and entertainment purposes only. All effort has been executed to present accurate, up to date, and reliable, complete information. No warranties of any kind are declared or implied. Readers acknowledge that the author is not engaging in the rendering of legal, financial, medical or professional advice. The content within this book has been derived from various sources. Please consult a licensed professional before attempting any techniques outlined in this book.

By reading this document, the reader agrees that under no circumstances is the author responsible for any losses, direct or indirect, which are incurred as a result of the use of information contained within this document, including, but not limited to, — errors, omissions, or inaccuracies.

Python Machine Learning

A Complete Guide for Beginners on Machine Learning and Deep Learning with Python

Table of Contents

INTRODUCTION **11**

WHAT IS MACHINE LEARNING? **15**

    APPLICATIONS OF MACHINE LEARNING 17
    ADVANTAGES AND DISADVANTAGES OF MACHINE LEARNING 20

MACHINE LEARNING - CONCEPTS & TERMS **23**

    MACHINE LEARNING, ARTIFICIAL INTELLIGENCE AND DEEP LEARNING 24
    OBJECTIVES OF MACHINE LEARNING SYSTEM 25
    CATEGORIES OF MACHINE LEARNING SYSTEMS 27
    STEPS IN BUILDING A MACHINE LEARNING SYSTEM 32

LINEAR REGRESSION WITH PYTHON **37**

    LINEAR REGRESSION WITH ONE VARIABLE 37

LISTS IN PYTHON **43**

    NESTED LISTS 43
    ACCESSING ELEMENTS FROM A LIST 44
    NESTED LIST INDEXING 45
    PYTHON NEGATIVE INDEXING 45
    SLICING LISTS IN PYTHON 46
    MANIPULATING ELEMENTS IN A LIST USING THE ASSIGNMENT OPERATOR .. 47
    CHANGING A RANGE OF ITEMS IN A LIST 48
    APPENDING/EXTENDING ITEMS IN THE LIST 48
    REMOVING OR DELETING ITEMS FROM A LIST 50
    DELETING MULTIPLE ELEMENTS 50
    USING EMPTY LIST TO DELETE AN ENTIRE OR SPECIFIC ELEMENTS 52
    SUMMARY OF LIST METHODS IN PYTHON 53
    INBUILT PYTHON FUNCTIONS TO MANIPULATE PYTHON LISTS 53

MODULES IN PYTHON **55**

    MODULES CONCEPT AND UTILITY WITHIN PYTHON 55
    HOW TO IMPORT A MODULE 57
    HOW TO WRITE AND USE A MODULE IN PYTHON? 61

MACHINE LEARNING TRAINING MODEL ... 69
SIMPLE MACHINE LEARNING TRAINING MODEL IN PYTHON ... 70
SIMPLE MACHINE LEARNING PYTHON MODEL USING LINEAR REGRESSION . 72

CONDITIONAL OR DECISION STATEMENTS ... 75
CONDITIONAL TESTS IN PYTHON ... 76
CHECKING EQUALITY ... 77
NUMERICAL COMPARISON IN PYTHON ... 78
CREATING MULTIPLE CONDITIONS ... 80
USING "AND" ... 80
USING "OR" ... 81
BOOLEAN EXPRESSIONS IN PYTHON ... 83
EXERCISES TO TRY ... 84
IF STATEMENTS ... 84
SIMPLE IF STATEMENTS ... 85
IF-ELSE STATEMENTS ... 87
THE IF-ELIF-ELSE CHAIN ... 89
MULTIPLE ELIF BLOCKS ... 91
PERFORMING MULTIPLE CONDITIONS ... 92
EXERCISE TO TRY ... 94

ESSENTIAL LIBRARIES FOR MACHINE LEARNING IN PYTHON ... 97
SCIKIT – LEARN ... 97
TENSORFLOW ... 98
THEANO ... 99
PANDAS ... 100
DIAGRAMMATIC EXPLANATIONS ... 100
MATPLOTLIB ... 101
DIAGRAMMATIC EXPLANATIONS ... 102
SEABORN ... 103
DIAGRAMMATIC ILLUSTRATIONS ... 104
NUMPY ... 105
SCIPY ... 105
KERAS ... 106
PYTORCH ... 107
SCRAPY ... 107

STATSMODELS 108

WHAT IS THE TENSORFLOW LIBRARY 109

INSTALLING TENSORFLOW 110
ACTIVATE TENSORENVIRON 115

ARTIFICIAL NEURAL NETWORKS 117

DEFINITION OF ARTIFICIAL NEURAL NETWORK... 117
EXAMPLE OF AN ARTIFICIAL NEURAL NETWORK 118
WHAT IS AN ACTIVATION FUNCTION AND ITS ROLE IN NEURAL NETWORK
MODELS? 119
THE SIGMOID FUNCTION 121
THE TANH FUNCTION 122
THE RELU FUNCTION 123
THE SOFTMAX FUNCTION... 125
WHAT ARE THE TYPES OF ARTIFICIAL NEURAL NETWORKS? 126
HOW TO TRAIN AN ARTIFICIAL NEURAL NETWORK? 128
ARTIFICIAL NEURAL NETWORK: PROS AND CONS OF USE 131

CONCLUSION 133

Introduction

For all that we know about Machine Learning, the truth is that we are nowhere close to realizing the true potential of these studies. Machine Learning is currently one of the hottest topics in computer science. If you are a data analyst, this is a field you should focus all your energy on because the prospects are incredible. You are looking at a future where interaction with machines will form the base of our being.

In this installation, our purpose was to address Python Machine Learning from the perspective of an expert. The assumption is that you have gone through the earlier books in the series that introduced you to Machine Learning, Python, libraries, and other important features that form the foundation of your knowledge in Machine Learning. With this in mind, we barely touched on the introductory concepts, unless necessary.

Even at an expert level, it is always important to remind yourself of the important issues that we must look at in Machine Learning. Algorithms are the backbone of almost everything that you will do in Machine Learning. Because of this reason, we introduced a brief section where you can remind yourself of the important algorithms and other elements that help you progress your knowledge of Machine Learning.

Machine Learning is as much about programming as it is about probability and statistics. There are many statistical approaches that we will use in Machine Learning to help us arrive at optimal solutions from time to time. It is therefore important that you remind yourself about some of the necessary probability theories and how they affect outcomes in each scenario.

In our studies of Machine Learning from the beginner books through an intermediary level to this point, one concept that stands out is that Machine Learning involves uncertainty. This is one of the differences between Machine Learning and programming. In programming, you write code that must be executed as it is written. The code derives a predetermined output based on the instructions given. However, in Machine Learning, this is not a luxury we enjoy.

Once you build the model, you train and test it and eventually deploy the model. Since these models are built to interact with humans, you can expect variances in the type of interaction that you experience at every level. Some input parameters might be correct, while others might not. When you build your model, you must consider these factors, or your model will cease to perform as expected.

The math element of Machine Learning is another area of study that we have to look at. We didn't touch on this so much in the earlier books in the series because it is an advanced level study. Many mathematical computations are involved in Machine Learning for the models to deliver the output we need. To support this cause, we must learn how to perform specific operations on data based on unique instructions.

As you work with different sets of data, there is always the possibility that you will come across massive datasets. This is normal because as our Machine Learning models interact with different users, they keep learning and build their knowledge. The challenge of using massive datasets is that you must learn how to break down the data into small units that your system can handle and process without any challenges. In this case, you are trying to avoid overworking your learning model.

Most basic computers will crash when they have to handle massive data. However, this should not be a problem when you learn how to fragment your datasets and perform computational operations on them.

At the beginning of this book, we mentioned that we will introduce hands-on approaches to using Machine Learning in daily applications. In light of this assertion, we looked at some practical methods of using Machine Learning, such as building a spam filter and analyzing a movie database.

We have taken a careful step-by-step approach to ensure that you can learn along the way, and more importantly, tried to explain each process to help you understand the operations you perform and why.

Eventually, when you build a Machine Learning model, the aim is to integrate it into some of the applications that people use daily. With this in mind, you must learn how to build a simple solution that addresses this challenge. We used simple explanations to help you understand this, and hopefully, as you keep working on different Machine Learning models, you can learn by building more complex models as your needs permit.

There are many concepts in Machine Learning that you will learn or come across over time. You must reckon the fact that this is a never-ending learning process as long as your model interacts with data. Over time, you will encounter greater datasets than those you are used to working with. In such a scenario, learning how to handle them will help you achieve your results faster, and without struggling.

What Is Machine Learning?

We live in a world where technology has become an inalienable part of our daily lives. In fact, with all the rapid changes in technology these days, machines enabled with artificial intelligence are now responsible for different tasks like prediction, recognition, diagnosis and so on.

Data are added or fed to the machines and these machines "learn" from these data. These data are referred to as training data because they are used to train the machines.

Once the machines have the data, they start to analyze any patterns present within the data and then perform actions based on these patterns. Machines use various learning mechanisms for analyzing the data according to the actions that they need to perform. These mechanisms can be broadly classified into two categories-supervised learning and unsupervised learning.

You might wonder why there aren't any machines designed solely to perform those tasks that they are needed to carry out. There are different reasons why Machine Learning is important. As already mentioned, all research conducted about Machine Learning comes in handy since it helps us understand a couple of aspects of human learning. Also, Machine Learning is quintessential because it helps increase the accuracy, effectiveness, and efficiency of machines.

Here is a real-life example that will help you understand this concept better.

Let us assume that there are two random users A and B who love listening to music and we have access to their history of songs. If you were a music company, then you can use Machine Learning to understand the kind of songs each of these users prefers and thereby you can come up with different ways in which you can sell your products to them.

For instance, you have access to noting down the different attributes of songs like their tempo, frequency or the gender of the voice, and then use all these attributes and plot a graph. Once you plot a graph, over time, it will become evident that A tends to prefer to listen to songs that have a fast tempo and are sung by male artists, whereas B likes to listen to slow songs sung by female artists, or any other similar insight. Once you obtain the data, you can transfer it to your marketing and advertising teams to make better product decisions.

At present, we have free access to all the historical data that has been collected since the advent of technology. Not only we do have access to these data, but we can now store and process such large quantities of data. Technology has certainly evolved, and it has come a long way when you look at the way we can now handle such operations. The technology is so refined these days that it provides access to more data to mine from.

Here are a couple of other reasons why Machine Learning is important.

Even with all the progress that engineers keep making, there will always be some tasks that are incapable of being defined explicitly.

Some tasks must be explained to the machines with the help of examples. The idea is to train the machine with the input of data and then teach it to process it to produce an output. In this manner, the machine will be aware of how it needs to deal with similar inputs of data in the future and process them accordingly to generate the appropriate outputs.

The fields of Machine Learning and data mining are intertwined. Data mining refers to the process of going through tons of data to find any bowlers correlations or relationships that exist within. This is another benefit of Machine Learning in the sense that it helps the machines find any vital information.

There are numerous occasions where humans can't design machines without having an accurate estimation of the conditions within which such machines will function.

The external conditions tend to have a major effect on the performance of the machine. In such situations, Machine Learning helps to get the machine acclimatized to its environment to ensure optimum performance. It also helps the machine to easily adapt to any changes in the environment without affecting its performance.

There is another problem if someone has to hardcode an extremely elaborate process into the machine, and then it is likely that the programmer will miss a couple of details. If there is any manual error, then it becomes quite tedious to encode all the details all over again. In such instances, it is better to allow the machine to learn the process instead.

The world of technology is in a constant flux of change and changes take place in the languages used as well. It isn't practical to keep redesigning the systems all over again to accommodate all the possible changes. Instead, Machine Learning helps the machine to automatically get acclimatized to all the changes.

Applications of Machine Learning

Machine Learning is drastically changing the way businesses are operated these days. It helps operate a large scale of data that's available and enables the users to draw helpful predictions based on the given information.

Certain manual tasks cannot be completed within a short time frame when large amounts of data are involved. Machine Learning is the answer to such problems. In the present times, we are overwrought with data and information and there is no physical way in which anyone can process all this information. Therefore, there is a dire need for an automated process and Machine Learning helps attain this objective.

When the processes of analysis and discovery are fully automated, it becomes simpler to attain useful information. This helps make all the future processes fully automated. The words Big Data, Business Analytics, and Data Science require Machine Learning. Predictive analytics and business intelligence are no longer restricted to just the elite businesses and are now accessible to small businesses and companies too. This allows small businesses to be a part of the process of collection and effective utilization of information. Let us look at a couple of technical applications of Machine Learning and see how these apply to problems in the real world.

Virtual Personal Assistants

Popular examples of virtual assistants available today are Alexa, Siri, and Google Now. As is obvious from the name, they help the user find the necessary information via voice commands. You simply need to activate it and then ask the question you want like, "What is my schedule for the day?" "What are the flights available between London and Germany?" or any other question that you want.

To answer your question, your personal assistant will look for information, recall the question you asked and then give you an answer. It can also be used to set reminders for certain tasks. Machine Learning is an important part of the process since it enables the system to gather and refine the information you need based on any of your previous involvements with it.

Density Estimation

Machine Learning allows the system to use the data that's available to it to suggest similar products. For instance, if you were to pick up a copy of Pride and Prejudice from a bookstore and then run it through a machine, then Machine Learning will help it determine the density of the words and come up with other books that are similar to Pride and Prejudice.

Latent Variables

When you are working with latent variables, the machine will use clustering to determine whether any of the variables present in it are related to one another or not. This comes in handy when you aren't certain of the reason that caused the change in variables and aren't aware of the relationship between the variables. When a large quantity of data is involved, it is easier to look for latent variables because it helps with a better understanding of the data thus obtained.

Reduction of Dimensionality

Usually, the data that is obtained tends to have some variables and dimensions. If there are more than three dimensions involved, then the human mind can't visualize that data. In such situations, Machine Learning helps to reduce these data into manageable proportions so that the user can easily understand the relationship between any variable.

Models of Machine Learning train the machines to learn from all the available data and offer different services like prediction or classification that in turn have multiple real-life applications like self-driving cars, the ability of smartphones to recognize the user's face or how Google Home or Alexa can recognize your accent and voice and how the accuracy of the machines improves if they have been learning for longer.

Advantages and Disadvantages of Machine Learning

The disadvantages of Machine Learning are:

1. In Machine Learning, we always train the model and then validate that model on a small data set. We then use that model to predict the output for some unseen or new data. You will find it difficult to identify if there was a bias in the model that you have created. If you cannot identify the bias, your inferences will be incorrect.

2. Some social scientists will begin to rely only on Machine Learning. It is important to remember that improvements should be made to some unsupervised Machine Learning tasks.

Some of the advantages of Machine Learning are:

1. Human beings cannot process large volumes of data, let

alone analyze that data. There is a lot of real-time data that is being produced, and if there is no automatic system to understand and analyze that data, we cannot reach any conclusion.

2. Machine Learning is getting better. With the advent of deep learning systems, the costs of data engineering and pre-processing of data are reducing.

Machine Learning - Concepts & Terms

Machine Learning is done by feeding the machine with relevant training data sets. Ordinary systems, that is, systems without any artificial intelligence, can always provide an output based on the input that is provided to the system. A system with artificial intelligence, however, can learn, predict and improve the results it provides through training.

Let us look at a simple example of how children learn to identify objects, or in other words how a child will associate a word with an object. Let us assume that there is a bowl of apples and oranges on the table. You, as an adult or parent, will introduce the round and red object as an apple, and the other object as an orange. In this example, the words apple and orange are labels, and the shapes and colors are attributes. You can also train a machine using a set of labels and attributes. The machine will learn to identify the object based on the attributes that are provided to it as input.

The models that are based on labeled training data sets are termed as supervised Machine Learning models. When children go to school, their teachers and professors give them some feedback about their progress. In the same way, a supervised Machine Learning model allows the engineer to provide some feedback to the machine.

Let us take an example of an input [red, round]. Here, both the child and machine will understand that any object which is round and red is an apple. Let us now place a cricket ball in front of either the machine or the child. You can feed the machine with the response negative 1 or 0 depending on whether the prediction is wrong or right. You can always add more attributes if necessary. This is the only way that a machine will learn. It is also for this reason that if you use a large-high-quality data set and spend more time training the machine, the machine will give you better and more accurate results.

Before we proceed further, you must understand the difference between the concepts of Machine Learning, artificial intelligence, and deep learning. Most people use these concepts interchangeably, but it is important to know that they are not the same.

Machine Learning, Artificial Intelligence and Deep Learning

The diagram below will give you an idea of how these terms relate.

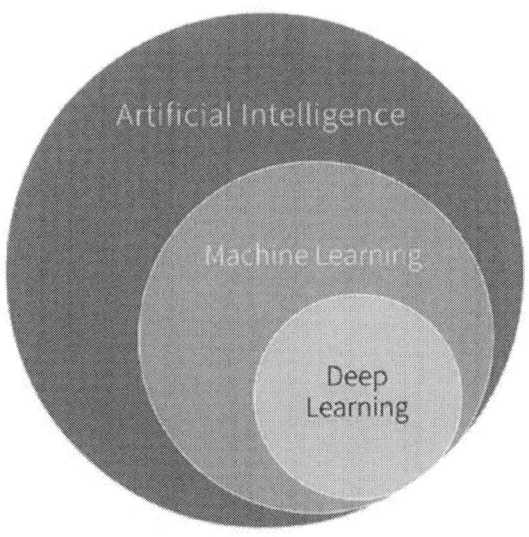

An illustration to understand the relationship between Machine Learning, Artificial Intelligence, and Deep Learning.

Artificial intelligence is a technique that is used to make machines mimic any human behavior. The aim is to ensure that a machine can accurately and efficiently mimic any human behavior. Some examples of artificial intelligence machines include deep blue chess and IBM's Watson.

Machine Learning, as defined above, is the use of statistical and mathematical models to help machines learned mimic human behavior. This is done using past data.

Deep learning is a subset of Machine Learning, and it refers to the functions and algorithms that an engineer uses to help a machine to train itself. The machine can learn to take the correct option to derive an output. Neural networks and natural language processing are a part of the deep learning ecosystem.

Objectives of Machine Learning System

The system of Machine Learning usually has one of the following objectives.

- Predict a category
- Predict a quantity
- Anomaly Detector Systems
- Clustering Systems

Predict a category

The model of Machine Learning helps analyze the input data and then predicts a category under which the output will fall. The prediction in such cases is usually a binary answer that's based on "yes" or "no". For instance, it helps with answers like, "will it rain today or not?" "is this a fruit?" "is this mail spam or not?" and so on. This is attained by referencing a group of data that will indicate whether a certain email falls under the category of spam or not based on specific keywords. This process is known as classification.

Predict a quantity

This system is usually used to predict a value like predicting the rainfall according to different attributes of the weather like the temperature, percentage of humidity, air pressure and so on. This sort of prediction is referred to as regression. The regression algorithm has various subdivisions like linear regression, multiple regression, etc.

Anomaly Detector Systems

The purpose of a model in anomaly detection is to detect any outliers in the given set of data. These applications are used in banking and e-commerce systems wherein the system is built to flag any unusual transactions. All this helps detect fraudulent transactions.

Clustering Systems

These forms of systems are still in the initial stages but their applications are numerous and can drastically change the way business is conducted. In this system, the user is classified into different clusters according to various behavioral factors like their age group, the region they live in or even the kind of programs they like to view. According to this clustering, the business can now suggest different programs or shows a user might be interested in watching according to the cluster that the said user belongs to during classification.

Categories of Machine Learning Systems

In the case of traditional machines, the programmer will give the machine a set of instructions and the input parameters, which the machine will use to compute make some calculations and derive an output using specific commands. In the case of Machine Learning systems, however, the system is never restricted by any command that the engineer provides, the machine will choose the algorithm that it can be used to process the data set and decide the output with high accuracy. It does this, by using the training data set which consists of historical data and output.

Therefore, in the classical world, we will tell the machine to process data based on a set of instructions, while in the Machine Learning error, we will never instruct a system. The computer will have to interact with the data set, develop an algorithm using the historical data set, make decisions like a human being would, analyze the information and then provide an output. The machine, unlike a human being, can process large data sets in short periods and provide results with high accuracy.

There are different types of Machine Learning algorithms, and they are classified based on the purpose of that algorithm. There are three categories in Machine Learning systems:

- Supervised Learning
- Unsupervised Learning
- Reinforced Learning

Supervised Learning

In this model, the engineers feed the machine with labeled data. In other words, the engineer will determine what the output of the system or specific data sets should be. This type of algorithm is also called a predictive algorithm. For example, consider the following table:

Currency (label)	Weight (Feature)
1 USD	10 gm
1 EUR	5 gm
1 INR	3 gm
1 RU	7 gm

In the above table, each currency is given an attribute of weight. Here, the currency is the label, and the weight is the attribute or feature.

The supervised Machine Learning system with first we fed with this training data set, and when it comes across any input of 3 grams, it will predict that the coin is a 1 INR coin. The same can be said for a 10-gram coin.

Classification and regression algorithms are a type of supervised

Machine Learning algorithms. Regression algorithms are used to predict match scores or house prices, while classification algorithms identify which category the data should belong to.

We will discuss some of these algorithms in detail in the later parts of the book, where you will also learn how to build or implement these algorithms using Python.

Unsupervised Learning

In this type of model, the system is more sophisticated in the sense that it will learn to identify patterns in unlabeled data and produce an output. This is a kind of algorithm that is used to draw any meaningful inference from large data sets. This model is also called the descriptive model since it uses data and summarizes that data to generate a description of the data sets. This model is often used in data mining applications that involve large volumes of unstructured input data.

For instance, if a system is Python input of name, runs and wickets, the system will visualize that data on a graph and identify the clusters. There will be two clusters generated - one cluster is for the batsman while the other is for the bowlers. When any new input is fed, the person will certainly fall into one of these clusters, which will help the machine predict whether the player is a batsman or a bowler.

Name	Runs	Wickets
Rachel	100	3
John	10	50

Paul	60	10
Sam	250	6
Alex	90	60

Sample data set for a match. Based on this the cluster model can group the players into batsmen or bowlers.

Some common algorithms which fall under unsupervised Machine Learning include density estimation, clustering, data reduction and compressing.

The clustering algorithm summarizes the data and presents it differently. This is a technique used in data mining applications. Density estimation is used when the objective is to visualize any large data set and create a meaningful summary. This will bring us the concept of data reduction and dimensionality. These concepts explain that the analysis or output should always deliver the summary of the data set without the loss of any valuable information. In simple words, these concepts say that the complexity of data can be reduced if the derived output is useful.

Reinforced learning

This type of learning is similar to how human beings learn, in the sense that the system will learn to behave in a specific environment, and take actions based on that environment. For example, human beings do not touch fire because they know it will hurt and they have been told that will hurt. Sometimes, out of curiosity, we may put a finger into the fire, and learn that it will burn. This means that we will be careful with fire in the future.

The table below will summarize and give an overview of the differences between supervised and unsupervised Machine Learning. This will also list the popular algorithms that are used in each of these models.

Supervised Learning	Unsupervised Learning
Works with labeled data	Works with unlabeled data
Takes Direct feedback	No feedback loop
Predicts output based on input data. Therefore also called "Predictive Algorithm"	Finds the hidden structure/pattern from input data. Sometimes called as "Descriptive Model"
Some common classes of supervised algorithms include: - Logistic Regression - Linear Regression (Numeric prediction) - Polynomial Regression - Regression trees (Numeric prediction) - Gradient Descent - Random Forest - Decision Trees (classification) - K-Nearest Algorithm (classification) - Naive Bayes - Support Vector Machines	Some common classes of unsupervised algorithms include: - Clustering, Compressing, density estimation & data reduction - K-means Clustering (Clustering) - Association Rules (Pattern Detection) - Singular Value Decomposition - Fuzzy Means - Partial Least Squares - Hierarchical Clustering - Principal Component Analysis

Table: Supervised vs Unsupervised Learning

We will look at each of these algorithms briefly and learn how to implement them in Python. Let us now look at some examples of where Machine Learning is applied. It is always a good idea to identify which type of Machine Learning model you must use with examples. The following points are explained in the next section:

- Facebook face recognition algorithm
- Netflix or YouTube recommending programs based on past viewership history
- Analyzing large volumes of bank transactions to guess if they are valid or fraudulent transactions.
- Uber's surge pricing algorithm

Steps in building a Machine Learning System

Regardless of the model of Machine Learning, here are the common steps that are involved in the process of designing a Machine Learning system.

Define Objective

As with any other task, the first step is to define the purpose you wish to accomplish with your system. The kind of data you use, the algorithm and other factors will primarily depend on the objective or the kind of prediction you want the system to produce.

Collect Data

This is perhaps the most time-consuming steps of building a system of Machine Learning. You must collect all the relevant data that you will use to train the algorithm.

Prepare Data

This is an important step that is usually overlooked. Overlooking this step can prove to be a costly mistake. The cleaner and the more relevant the data you are using is, the more accurate the prediction or the output will be.

Select Algorithm

There are different algorithms that you can choose, like Structured Vector Machine (SVM), k-nearest, Naive-Bayes, Apriori, etc. The algorithm that you use will primarily depend on the objective you wish to attain with the model.

Train Model

Once you have all the data ready, you must feed it into the machine and the algorithm must be trained to predict.

Test Model

Once your model is trained, it is now ready to start reading the input to generate appropriate outputs.

Predict

Multiple iterations will be performed and you can also feed the feedback into the system to improve its predictions over time.

Deploy

Once you test the model and are satisfied with the way it is working, the said model will be sterilized and can be integrated into any application you want. This means that it is ready to be deployed.

All these steps can vary according to the application and the type of algorithm (supervised or unsupervised) you are using. However, these steps are generally involved in all processes of designing a system of Machine Learning. There are various languages and tools that you can use in each of these stages. In this book, you will learn about how you can design a system of Machine Learning using Python.

Let us understand the scenarios from the previous section below.

Scenario One

In a picture from a tagged album, Facebook recognizes the photo of the friend.

Explanation: This is an instance of supervised learning. In this case, Facebook is using tagged photographs to recognize the person. The tagged photos will become the labels of the pictures. Whenever a machine is learning from any form of labeled data, it is referred to as supervised learning.

Scenario Two

Suggesting new songs based on someone's past music preferences.

Explanation: This is an instance of supervised learning. The model is training classified or pre-existing labels- in this case, the genre of songs. This is precisely what Netflix, Pandora, and Spotify do – they collect the songs/movies that you like, evaluate the features based on your preferences and then come up with suggestions of songs or movies based on similar features.

Scenario Three

Analyzing the bank data to flag any suspicious or fraudulent transactions.

Explanation: This is an instance of unsupervised learning. The suspicious transaction cannot be fully defined in this case and therefore, there are no specific labels like fraud or not a fraud. The model will try to identify any outliers by checking for anomalous transactions.

Scenario Four

Combination of various models.

Explanation: The surge pricing feature of Uber is a combination of different models of Machine Learning like the prediction of peak hours, the traffic in specific areas, the availability of cabs and clustering is used to determine the usage pattern of users in different areas of the city.

Linear Regression with Python

Linear regression with one variable

The first part of linear regression that we are going to focus on is when we just have one variable. This is going to make things a bit easier to work with and will ensure that we can get some of the basics down before we try some of the things that are a bit harder. We are going to focus on problems that have just one independent and one dependent variable on them.

To help us get started with this one, we are going to use the set of data for car_price.csv so that we can learn what the price of the care is going to be. We will have the price of the car be our dependent variable and then the year of the car is going to be the independent variable. You can find this information in the folders for Data sets that we talked about before. To help us make a good prediction on the price of the cars, we will need to use the Scikit Learn library from Python to help us get the right algorithm for linear regression. When we have all of this setup, we need to use the following steps to help out.

Importing the right libraries

First, we need to make sure that we have the right libraries to get this going. The codes that you need to get the libraries for this section include:

```
import pandas as pd
import numpy as np
import matplotlib.pyplot as plt
%matplotlib inline
```

You can implement this script into the Jupyter notebook. The final line needs to be there if you are using the Jupyter notebook, but if you are using Spyder, you can remove the last line because it will go through and do this part without your help.

Importing the Dataset

Once the libraries have been imported using the codes that you had before, the next step is going to be importing the data sets that you want to use for this training algorithm. We are going to work with the "car_price.csv" dataset. You can execute the following script to help you get the data set in the right place:

```
car_data = pd.read_csv('D:\Datasets\car_price.csv')
```

Analyzing the data

Before you use the data to help with training, it is always best to practice and analyze the data for any scaling or any values that are missing. First, we need to take a look at the data. The head function is going to return the first five rows of the data set you want to bring up. You can use the following script to help make this one work:

```
car_data.head()
```

Also, the described function can be used to return to you all of the statistical details of the dataset.

```
car_data.describe ()
```

Finally, let's take a look to see if the linear regression algorithm is going to be suitable for this kind of task. We are going to take the data points and plot them on the graph. This will help us to see if there is a relationship between the year and the price. To see if this will work out, use the following script:

```
plt.scatter(car_data['Year'], car_data['Price'])
plt.title("Year vs Price")
plt.xlabel("Year")
plt.ylabel("Price")
plt.show()
```

When we use the above script, we are trying to work with a scatterplot that we can then find on the library Matplotlib. This is going to be useful because this scatter plot is going to have the year on the x-axis and then the price is going to be over on our y-axis. From the figure for the output, we can see that when there is an increase in the year, then the price of the car is going to go up as well. This shows us the linear relationship that is present between the year and the price. This is a good way to see how this kind of algorithm can be used to solve this problem.

Going back to data pre-processing

Now we need to use that information and have these two tasks come up for us. To divide the data into features and labels, you will need to use the script below to get it started:

```
features = car_data.iloc[:,0:1].values
labels = car_data.iloc[:,1].values
```

Since we only have two columns here, the 0TH column is going to contain the feature set and then the first column is going to contain the label. We will then be able to divide up the data so that there are 20 percent to the test set and 80 percent to the training. Use the following scripts to help you get this done:

```
from sklearn.model_selection import train_test_split
```

```
train_features, test_features, train_labels
test_labels = train_test_split (features, labels,
test_size = 0.2, random_state = 0)
```

From this part, we can go back and look at the set of data again. And when we do this, it is easy to see that there is not going to be a huge difference between the values of the years and the values of the prices. Both of these will end up being in the thousands each. What this means is that you don't need to do any scaling because you can just use the data as you have it here. That saves you some time and effort in the long run.

How to train the algorithm and get it to make some predictions

Now it is time to do a bit of training with the algorithm and ensure that it can make the right predictions for you. This is where the LinearRegression class is going to be helpful because it has all of the labels and other training features that you need to input and train your models. This is simple to do and you just need to work with the script below to help you to get started:

```
from sklearn.linear_model import LinearRegresison
lin_reg = LinearRegression()
lin_reg.fit (train_features, train_labels)
```

Using the same example of the car prices and the years from before, we are going to look and see what the coefficient is for only the independent variable. We need to use the following script to help us do that:

```
print(lin_reg.coef_)
```

The result of this process is going to be 204.815. This shows that for each unit change in the year, the car price is going to increase by 204.815 (at least in this example).

Once you have taken the time to train this model, the final step to use is to predict the new instance that you are going to work with. The predict method is going to be used with this kind of class to help see this happen. The method is going to take the test features that you choose and add them in as the input, and then it can predict the output that would correspond with it the best. The script that you can use to make this happen will be the following:

```
predictions = lin_reg.predict( test_features)
```

When you use this script, you will find that it is going to give us a good prediction of what we are going to see in the future. We can guess how much a car is going to be worth based on the year it is produced in the future, going off the information that we have right now. There could be some things that can change with the future, and it does seem to matter based on the features that come with the car. But this is a good way to get a look at the cars and get an average of what they cost each year, and how much they will cost in the future.

So, let's see how this would work. We now want to look at this linear regression and figure out how much a car is going to cost us in the year 2025. Maybe you would like to save up for a vehicle and you want to estimate how much it is going to cost you by the time you save that money. You would be able to use the information that we have and add in the new year that you want it based on, and then figure out an average value for a new car that year.

Of course, remember that this is not going to be 100 percent accurate. Inflation could change prices, the manufacturer may change some things up, and more. Sometimes the price is going to be lower, and sometimes higher. But it at least gives you a good way to predict the price of the vehicle that you have and how much it is going to cost you in the future.

Lists In Python

We create a list in Python by placing items called elements inside square brackets separated by commas. The items in a list can be of mixed data types.

Start IDLE.

Navigate to the File menu and click New Window.

Type the following:

```
list_mine=[] #empty list
list_mine=[2,5,8] #list of integers
list_mine=[5,"Happy", 5.2] #list having mixed data types
```

Exercise

Write a program that captures the following in a list: "Best", 26, 89, 3.9

Nested Lists

A nested list is a list as an item in another list.

Example

Start IDLE.

Navigate to the File menu and click New Window.

Type the following:

```
list_mine=["carrot", [9, 3, 6], ['g']]
```

Exercise

Write a nested list for the following elements: [36, 2, 1], "Writer", 't', [3.0, 2.5]

Accessing Elements from a List

In Python, the first time is always indexed as zero. A list of five items can be accessed by index0 to index4. An index error will occur if you fail to access the items in a list. The index is always an integer, so using other numbers will also create a type error.

Example

Start IDLE.

Navigate to the File menu and click New Window.

Type the following:

```
list_mine=['b','e','s','t']
print(list_mine[0])#the output will be b
print(list_mine[2])#the output will be s
print(list_mine[3])#the output will be t
```

Exercise

Given the following list:

```
your_collection=['t','k','v','w','z','n','f']
```

a. Write a Python program to display the second item in the list

b. Write a Python program to display the sixth item in the last

c. Write a Python program to display the last item in the list.

Nested List Indexing

Start IDLE.

Navigate to the File menu and click New Window.

Type the following:

```
nested_list=["Best',[4,7,2,9]]
print(nested_list[0][1])
```

Python Negative Indexing

For its sequences, Python allows negative indexing. The last item on the list is index-1, index -2 is the second last item and so on.

Start IDLE.

Navigate to the File menu and click New Window.

Type the following:

```
list_mine=['c','h','a','n','g','e','s']
```

```
print(list_mine[-1])#Output is s
print(list_mine [-4])##Output is n
```

Slicing Lists in Python

Slicing operator (full colon) is used to access a range of elements in a list.

Example

Start IDLE.

Navigate to the File menu and click New Window.

Type the following:

```
list_mine=['c','h','a','n','g','e','s']
print(list_mine[3:5]) #Picking elements from the fourth to the sixth
```

Example

Picking elements from start to the fifth

Start IDLE.

Navigate to the File menu and click New Window.

Type the following:

```
print(list_mine[:-6])
```

Example

Picking the third element to the last

```
print(list_mine[2:])
```

Exercise

Given class_names = ['John', 'Kelly', 'Yvonne', 'Una', 'Lovy', 'Pius', 'Tracy']

a. Write a Python program using the slice operator to display from the second students and the rest.

b. Write a Python program using the slice operator to display the first student to the third using the negative indexing feature.

c. Write a Python program using the slice operator to display the fourth and fifth students only.

Manipulating Elements in a List using the Assignment Operator

Items in a list can be changed, meaning lists are mutable.

Start IDLE.

Navigate to the File menu and click New Window.

Type the following:

```
list_yours=[4,8,5,2,1]
list_yours[1]=6
print(list_yours) #The output will be [4,6,5,2,1]
```

Changing a Range of Items in a List

Start IDLE.

Navigate to the File menu and click New Window.

Type the following:

```
list_yours[0:3]=[12,11,10] #Will change first item to fourth item in the list
print(list_yours) #Output will be: [12,11,10,1]
```

Appending/Extending Items in the List

The `append()` method allows extending the items in the list. The `extend()` can also be used.

Example

Start IDLE.

Navigate to the File menu and click New Window.

Type the following:

```
list_yours=[4, 6, 5]
list_yours.append(3)
print(list_yours)#The output will be [4,6,5, 3]
```

Example

Start IDLE.

Navigate to the File menu and click New Window.

Type the following:

```
list_yours=[4,6,5]
list_yours.extend([13,7,9])
print(list_yours)#The output will be [4,6,5,13,7,9]
```

The plus operator (+) can also be used to combine two lists. The * operator can be used to iterate a list a given number of times.

Example

Start IDLE.

Navigate to the File menu and click New Window.

Type the following:

```
list_yours=[4,6,5]
print(list_yours+[13,7,9])# Output:[4, 6, 5,13,7,9]
print(['happy']*4)#Output:["happy","happy",
"happy","happy"]
```

Removing or Deleting Items from a List

The keyword `del` is used to delete elements or the entire list in Python.

Example

Start IDLE.

Navigate to the File menu and click New Window.

Type the following:

```
list_mine=['t','r','o','g','r','a','m']
del list_mine[1]
print(list_mine) #t, o, g, r, a, m
```

Deleting Multiple Elements

Example

Start IDLE.

Navigate to the File menu and click New Window.

Type the following:

```
del list_mine[0:3]
```

Example

```
print(list_mine) #a, m
```

Delete Entire List

Start IDLE.

Navigate to the File menu and click New Window.

Type the following:

```
delete list_mine
print(list_mine) #will generate an error of lost not found
```

The remove() method or pop() method can be used to remove the specified item. The pop() method will remove and return the last item if the index is not given and helps implement lists as stacks. The clear() method is used to empty a list.

Example

Start IDLE.

Navigate to the File menu and click New Window.

Type the following:

```
list_mine=['t','k','b','d','w','q','v']
list_mine.remove('t')
print(list_mine)#output will be
['t','k','b','d','w','q','v']
```

```
print(list_mine.pop(1))#output will be 'k'
print(list_mine.pop())#output will be 'v'
```

Exercise

Given list_yours=['K','N','O','C','K','E','D']

a. Pop the third item in the list, save the program as list1.

b. Remove the fourth item using remove() method and save the program as list2

c. Delete the second item in the list and save the program as list3.

d. Pop the list without specifying an index and save the program as list4.

Using Empty List to Delete an Entire or Specific Elements

Start IDLE.

Navigate to the File menu and click New Window.

Type the following:

```
list_mine=['t','k','b','d','w','q','v']
list_mine=[1:2]=[]
print(list_mine)#Output will be ['t','w','q','v']
```

Summary of List Methods in Python

Method	Description	Method	Description
insert()	- Insert an item at the defined index	copy()	- Returns a shallow copy of the list
append()	- Add an element to the end of the list	count()	- Returns the count of number of items passed as an argument
pop()	- Removes and returns an element at the given index	clear()	- Removes all items from the list
index()	- Returns the index of the first matched item	sort()	- Sort items in a list in ascending order
remove()	- Removes an item from the list	extend()	- Add all elements of a list to the another list
		reverse()	- Reverse the order of items in the list

Inbuilt Python Functions to Manipulate Python Lists

Method	Description	Method	Description
enumerate()	Return an enumerate object and contains the index and value of all the items of list as a tuple.	len()	Return the length in the list.
sorted()	Return a new sorted list but does not sort the list itself	any()	Return True if any element of the list is true. If the list is empty, return False.
sum()	Return the sum of all elements in the list.	min()	Return the smallest item in the list
max()	Return the largest item in the list.	all()	Return True if all elements of the list are true

Exercise

Use list access methods to display the following items in reversed order list_yours=[4,9,2,1,6,7]

Use the list access method to count the elements in list_yours.

Use the list access method to sort the items in list_yours in an ascending order/default.

Modules In Python

Modules, also known as packages, are a set of names. This is usually a library of functions and/or object classes that are made available to be used within different programs. We used the notion of modules earlier in this chapter to use some function from the math library. In this chapter, we are going to cover in-depth on how to develop and define modules. To use modules in a Python program, the following statements are used: import, from, reload. The first one imports the whole module. The second allows import only a specific name or element from the module. The third one, reload, allows reloading a code of a module while Python is running and without stopping in it. Before digging into their definition and development, let's start first by the utility of modules or packages within Python.

Modules Concept and Utility Within Python

Modules are a very simple way to make a system component organized. Modules allow reusing the same code over and over. So far, we were working in a Python interactive session. Every code we have written and tested is lost once we exit the interactive session. Modules are saved in files that make them persistent, reusable, and sharable. You can consider modules as a set of files where you can define functions, names, data objects, attributes, and so on. Modules are a tool to group several components of a system in a single place. In Python programming, modules are among the highest-level unit. They point to the name of packages and tools. Besides, they allow the sharing of the implemented data. You only need one copy of the module to be able to use across a large program. If an object is to be used in different functions and programs, coding it as a module allows share it with other programmers.

To have a sense of the architecture of Python coding, we go through some general structure explanation. We have been using so far in this book very simple code examples that do not have high-level structure. In large applications, a program is a set of several Python files. By Python files, we mean files that contain Python code and have a .py extension. There is one main high-level program and the other files are the modules. The high-level file consists of the main code that dictates the control flow and executes the application. Module files define the tools that are needed to process elements and components of the main program and maybe elsewhere. The main program makes use of the tools that are specified in the modules.

In their turn, modules make use of tools that are specified in other modules. When you import a module in Python, you have access to every tool that is declared or defined in that specific module. Attributes are the variables or the functions associated with the tools within a module. Hence, when a module is imported, we have access to the attributes of the tools as well to process them. For instance, let's consider we have two Python files named file1.py and file2.py where the file1.py is the main program and file2.py is the module. In the file2.py, we have a code that defines the following function:

```
def Xfactorial (X):
P = 1
for i in range (1, X + 1):
P *= i
return P
```

To use this function in the main program, we should define code statements in the file1.py as follows:

```
Import file2
A = file2.Xfactorial (3)
```

The first line imports the module file2.py. This statement means to load the file file2.py. This gives access to the file1.py to all tools and functions defined in file2.py by the name file2. The function Xfactorial is called by the second line. The module file2.py is where this function is defined using the attributes' syntax. The line file2.Xfactorial() means fetch any name value of Xfactorial and lies within the code body of file2. In this example, it is a function that is callable. So, we have provided an input argument and assigned the output result to the variable A. If we add a third statement to print the variable A and run the file file1.py, it would display 6 which is the factorial of 3. Along Python, you will see the attribute syntax as object.attribute. This allows calling the attributes that might be a function or data object that provides properties of the object.

Note that some modules that you might import when programming with Python are available in Python itself. As we have mentioned at the beginning of this book, Python comes with a standard large library that has built-in modules. These modules support all common tasks that might be needed in programming from operating system interfaces to graphical user interface. They are not part of the language. However, they can be imported and comes with a software installation package. You can check the complete list of available modules in a manual that comes with the installation or goes to the official Python website: www.Python.org. This manual is kept updated every time a new version of Python is released.

How to Import a Module

We have talked about importing a module without really explaining what happens behind in Python. Imports are a very fundamental concept in Python programming structure. In this section, we are going to cover in-depth how really Python imports modules within a program. Python follows three steps to import a file or a module within the work environment of a program. The first step consists of finding the file that contains the module. The second step consists of compiling the module to a byte-code if required. Finally, the third step runs the code within the module file to build the objects that are defined. These three steps are run only when the module is imported for the first time during the execution of a program. This module and all its objects are loaded in the memory. When the module is imported further in the program, it skips all three steps and just fetch the objects defined by the module and are saved in memory.

At the very first step of importing a module, Python has to find the module file location. Note that, so far in the examples we presented, we used import without providing the complete path of the module or extension .py. We just used import math, or import file2.py (an example of the previous section). Python import statement omits the extension and the path. We just simply import a module by its name. The reason for this is that Python has a module that looks for paths called 'search path module'. This module is used specifically to find the path of module files that are imported by the import statements.

In some cases, you might need to configure the path search of modules to be able to use new modules that are not part of the standard library. You need to customize it to include these new modules. The search path is simply the concatenation of the home directory, directories of PYTHONPATH, directories of the standard library, and optionally if the content of files with extension .pth when they exist. The home directory is set automatically by the system to a directory of Python executable when launched from the interactive session, or it can be modified to the working directory where your program is saved. This directory is the first to be searched when import a module is run without a path. Hence, if your home directory points to a directory that includes your program along with the modules, importing these modules does not require any path specification.

The directory of the standard library is also searched automatically. This directory contains all default libraries that come with Python. The directories of PYTHONPATH can be set to point toward the directory of new modules that are developed. In fact, PTYHONPATH is an environment variable that contains a list of directories that contains Python files. When PTYHONPATH is set, all these paths are included in the Python environment and the search path directory would search these directories too when importing modules. Python also allows defining a file with .pth extension that contains directories, one in each line. This file serves the same as PTYHONPATH when included appropriately in a directory. You can check the directories' paths included when you run Python using sys.path. You simply print sys.path to get the list of the directories that Python will be searching for.

Remember, when importing a module, we just use the name of the module without its extension. When Python is searching for a module in its environment paths, it selects the first name that matches the module name regardless of the extension. Because Python allows using packages that are coded in other languages, it does not simply select a module with .py extension but a file name or even a zip file name that matches the module name being imported. Therefore, you should name your modules distinctly and configure the search path in a manner that makes it obvious to choose a module.

When Python finds the source code of the module file with a name that corresponds to the name in the import statement, it will compile it into byte code in case it is required. This step is skipped if

Python finds an already byte code file with no source code. If the source code has been modified, another byte code file is automatically regenerated by Python while the program runs in other further executions. Byte code files have typically .pyc extension. When Python is searching and finds the module file name, it will load the byte code file that corresponds to the latest version of the source code with .py extension. If the source code is newer than the byte code file, it will generate a new one by compiling the source code file. Note that only imported files have corresponding files with .pyc extension. These files, the byte code files, are stored on your machine to make the imports faster in future use.

The third step of the import statement is running the module's byte code. Each statement and each assignment in the file are executed. This allows generating any function, data objects, and so on defined in the module. The functions and all attributes are accessed within the program via importers. During this step, you will see print statements if they exist. The 'def ' statement will create a function object to be used in the main program.

To summarize the import statement, it involves searching for the file, compiling it, and running the byte code file. All other import statements use the module stored in memory and ignore all the three steps. When first imported, Python will look in the search path module to select the module. Hence, it is important to configure correctly the path environment variable to point to the directory that contains new defined modules. Now that you have the big picture and the concept of modules, let's explore how we can define and develop new modules.

How to write and use a module in Python?

Modules in Python can be created very easily and do not require any specific syntax. Modules are simply files with a .py extension that contains Python code. You can use a text editor like Notepad++ to develop and write modules then save them in files with the .py extension. Then, you just import these files like we have seen in the previous section to make use of the contained code.

When you create a module, all the data object including functions that are defined becomes the module attributes. These attributes are accessed and used via the attribute syntax like follows: module.attribute. For instance, if we define a module named ' MyModule.py ' that has the following function:

```
def Myfct (A):
print (' A by 2 is: ', A * 2)
return A * 2
```

The function ' Myfct ' becomes the attribute of the module ' MyModule.py '. You can call a module any Python code that you develop and save in a file with a .py extension if you are importing them in later use. Module names are referenced variables. Hence, when naming a module, you should follow the same rules as for variable naming. You might be able to name your module anything you want. But if the rules are not respected, Python throws an error. For instance, if you name your module $2P.py, you will not be able to import it and Python would trigger a syntax error. Directory names that contain the module and Python packages should follow the same rules. Also, their names cannot contain any space. In the rest of this section, we are going to provide some code examples of defining and using modules.

Two statements can be employed to make use of a module. The first one is the import statement we have covered in the previous section. Let's consider again the previous example to illustrate a module 'MyModule.py' that contains ' Myfct' function:

```
def Myfct(A):
print (A, 'by 2 is: ', A * 2)
```

Now, to use this module, we import it using the following statements:

```
>>> import MyModule
>>> MyModule.Myfct(2)
2 by 2 is: 4
```

Now, the MyModule name is being used by Python to load the file and as a variable in the program. The module name should be used to access all its attributes. Another way to import and use a module attribute is by using the 'from import' statement. This statement works in the same manner as the import statement we have been using. Instead of using the module name to fetch for its attributes, we can access the attributes by their names directly. For example:

```
>>> from MyModule import Myfct
>>> Myfct (2)
2 by 2 is: 4
```

This statement makes a copy of the function name without using the module name. There is another form of 'from import' statement that uses an *. This statement allows copying all names that are assigned to objects in the module. For example:

```
>>> from MyModule import *
```

```
>>> Myfct (2)
2 by 2 is: 4
```

Because modules names become variables (i.e. references to objects), Python supports importing a module with an alias. Then we can access its attributes using the alias instead of its name. For instance, we can attribute an alias to our module as follows:

```
>>> import Mymodule as md
>>> md.Myfct(2)
2 by 2 is: 4
```

Data objects other than functions are accessed the same way with attribute syntax. For instance, we can define and initialize data objects in modules than used them later in the program. Let's consider the following code to create a module named ExModule.py.

```
A = 9
Name = 'John'
```

In this example, we initialize both variables A and Name. Now, after importing the module, we can get both variables as follows:

```
>>> import ExModule
>>> print ('A is: ', ExModule.A)
A is: 9
>>> print ('Name is: ', Exmodule.Name)
Name is: John
```

Or we can assign attributes to other variables. For instance:

```
>>> import ExModule
>>> B = ExModule.A
>>> print ('B is: ', B)
B is: 9
```

If we use the 'from import' statement to import the attributes, the names of the attributes become variables in the script. For example:

```
>>> from Exmodule import A, Name
>>> print ('A is: ', A, 'and Name is: ', Name)
```
A is 9 and Name is John

Note that the 'from import' statement supports importing multiple attributes in one single line. Python allows changing objects that are sharable. For instance, let's consider the following code to define the module named ExModul1.py:

```
A = 9
MyList = [90, 40, 80]
```

Now, let's import this module and try to change the values of the attributes to see how Python behaves.

```
>>> from ExModule1 import A, MyList
>>> A = 20
>>> myList [0] = 100
```

Now, let's re-import the module and print those two attributes and see what changes Python has made.

```
>>> import ExModule1
>>> print ('A is: ', ExModule1.A)
A is: 9
>>> print ('My list is: ', ExModule.myList)
My list is: [100, 40, 80]
```

You can notice that Python has changed the value of the first element of the list but did not change the value of the variable 'A' to the value we assigned before. The reason is that when a mutable object like lists is changed locally, the changes apply also in the module from which they were imported. Reassigning a fetched variable name does not reassign the reference in the module from which it was imported. In fact, there is no link between the reference variable name copied and the file it was copied from. To make a valid modification in the script and the module it is imported from, we should use the import statement like follows:

```
>>> import ExModule1
>>> ExModule1.A = 200
```

The difference between changing the attributes 'A' and 'myList' is the fact that 'A' is a variable name and 'myList' is an object data. That is why modification to the variable 'A' should use import to be applied in the module file, too.

We have mentioned that importing a module for the first time in a script implies going through three steps that are searching for the module, compiling the module, and running the module. All other imports of the module later in the script skip all these three steps and access to module loaded in the memory. Now, let's try an example to see how this works. Consider we have a module with the following code and named ExModule2.py:

```
print (' Hello World\n')
print (' This is my first module in Python')
A = 9
```

Now, let's import this module and see how Python behaves when importing this module:

```
>>> import ExModule2
Hello World
This is my first module in Python
```

You can notice that when importing this module, it displays both messages. Now, let's try to reassign a value to the attribute ' A', then re-import the module with the import statement.

```
>>> ExModule.A = 100
>>> import Exmodule2
```

As you can note from the example, Python did not display the messages, ' Hello World' and ' This is my first module in Python' because it did not re-run the module. It just used the module that is already loaded in the memory.

To make Python goes through all steps of importing a module for the second time in a script, we should use the reload statement. When using this statement, we force Python to import the module as it would for the first time. Besides, it helps make modifications in the program while it is running without interrupting it. It also helps see instantly the modifications that are made. The reload is a function and not a statement in Python that takes as argument a module that is already loaded in memory.

Because reload is a function and expects an argument, this argument should be already assigned an object which is a module object. If for some reason the import statement failed to import a module, you will not be able to reload it. You have to repeat the import statement until it imports the module successfully. Like any other function, the reload takes the module name reference between parentheses. The general form of using reload with import is as follows:

```
import module_name
list of statements that use module attributes
reload(module_name)
list of statements that use module attributes
```

The module object is changed by the reload function. Hence, any reference to that module in your scripts is impacted by the reload function. Those statements that use the module attributes will be using the values of the new attributes if they are modified. The reload function overwrites the module source code and re-runs it instead of deleting the file and creating a new one. In the following code example, we will see a concrete illustration of the reload functioning. We consider the following code to create a module named ExModule3.py:

```
my_message = 'This is my module first version'
def display ():
print (my_message)
```

This module simply assigns a string to the variable 'my_message' and print it. Now, let's import this module in Python and call the attribute function:

```
>>> import ExModule3
>>> Exmodule3.display()
This is my module first version
```

Now, go to your text editor and edit the module source code without stopping the Python prompt shell. You can make a change as follows:

my_message = 'This is my module second version edited in the text editor'

def display ():

print (my_message)

Now, back to the interactive session of Python in the prompt shell, you can try to import the module and call the function:

```
>>> import ExModule3
```

```
>>> Exmodule3.display()
This is my module first version
```

As you can notice that the message did not change although the source code file was modified. As said before, all imports after the first import use the already loaded module in memory. To get the new message and access the modification made in the module, we use the reload function:

```
>>> reload (ExModule3)
<module 'ExModule3)>
>>> Exmodule3.display()
This is my module second version edited in the text editor
```

Note that the reload function re-runs module and returns the module object. Because it was executed in the interactive session, it displays < module name> by default.

Machine Learning Training Model

In Machine Learning, a model is a mathematical or digital representation of a real-world process. To build a good Machine Learning (ML) model, developers need to provide the right training data to an algorithm. An algorithm, on the other hand, is a hypothetical set taken before training begins with real-world data.

A linear regression algorithm, for example, is a set of functions defining similar characteristics or features as defined by linear regression. Developers choose the function that fits most of the training data from a set or group of functions. The process of training for Machine Learning involves providing an algorithm with training data.

The basic purpose of creating any ML model is to expose it to a lot of inputs, as well as the output applicable to it, allowing it to analyze these data and use it to determine the relationship between them and the results. For example, if a person wants to decide whether to carry an umbrella or not depending on the weather, he/she will need to look at the weather conditions, which, in this case, is the training data.

Professional data scientists spend more of their time and effort on the steps preceding the following processes:

1. Data exploration

2. Data cleaning

3. Engineering new features

Simple Machine Learning Training Model in Python

When it comes to Machine Learning, having the right data is more important than having the ability to write a fancy algorithm. A good modeling process will protect against over-fitting and maximize performance. In Machine Learning, data are a limited resource, which developers should spend doing the following:

1. Feeding their algorithm or training their model
2. TESTING THEIR MODEL

However, they cannot reuse the same data to perform both functions. If they do this, they could over-fit their model and they would not even know. The effectiveness of a model depends on its ability to predict unseen or new data; therefore, it is important to have separate training and test different sections of the dataset. The primary aim of using training sets is to fit and fine-tune one's model. Test sets, on the other hand, are new datasets for the evaluation of one's model.

Before doing anything else, it is important to split data to get the best estimates of the model's performance. After doing this, one should avoid touching the test sets until one is ready to choose the final model. Comparing training versus test performance allows developers to avoid over-fitting. If a model's performance is adequate or exceptional on the training data but inadequate on the test data, then the model has this problem.

In the field of Machine Learning, over-fitting is one of the most important considerations. It describes how well the target function's approximation correlates with the training data provided. It happens when the training data provided has a high signal to noise ratio, which will lead to poor predictions.

Essentially, an ML model is over-fitting if it fits the training data exceptionally well while generalizing new data poorly. Developers overcome this problem by creating a penalty on the model's parameters, thereby limiting the model's freedom.

When professionals talk about tuning models in Machine Learning, they usually mean working on hyper-parameters. In Machine Learning, there are two main types of parameters, i.e., model parameters and hyper-parameters. The first type defines individual models and is a learned attribute, such as decision tree locations and regression coefficients.

The second type, however, defines higher-level settings for Machine Learning algorithms, such as the number of trees in a random forest algorithm or the strength of the penalty used in regression algorithms.

The process of training a machine-learning model involves providing an algorithm with training data. The term machine-learning model refers to the model artifact created by the ML training process. Data should contain the right answer, known as the target attribute. The algorithm looks for patterns in the data that point to the answer it wants to predict and creates a model that captures these different patterns.

Developers can use machine-learning models to generate predictions on new data for which they do not know the target attributes. Supposing a developer wanted to train a model to predict whether an email is legitimate or spam, for example, he/she would give it training data containing emails with known labels that define the emails as either spam or not spam. Using these data to train the model will result in trying to predict whether a new email is legitimate or spam.

Simple Machine Learning Python Model using Linear Regression

When it comes to building a simple ML model in Python, beginners need to download and install sci-kit-learn, an open-source Python library with a wide variety of visualization, cross-validation, pre-processing, and Machine Learning algorithms using a unified user-interface. It offers easy-to-understand and use functions designed to save a significant amount of time and effort. Developers also need to have Python Version 3 installed in their system.

Some of the most important features of sci-kit-learn include;

1. Efficient and easy-to-use tools for data analysis and data mining

2. BSD license

3. Reusable in many different contexts and highly accessible

4. Built on the top of matplotlib, SciPy, and NumPy

5. Functionality for companion tasks

6. Excellent documentation

7. Tuning parameters with sensible defaults

8. User-interface supporting various ML models

Before installing this library, users need to have SciPy and NumPy installed. If they already have a data set, they need to split it into training data, testing data, and validation data. However, in this example, they are creating their own training set, which will contain both the input and desired output values of the data set they want to use to train their model. To load an external dataset, they can use the Panda library, which will allow them to easily load and manipulate datasets.

Their input data will consist of random integer values, which will generate a random integer N; for instance, a <= N <= b. As such, they will create a function that will determine the output. Recall a function uses some input value to return some output value. Having created their training set, they will split each row into an input training set and its related output training set, resulting in two lists of all inputs and their corresponding outputs.

Benefits of splitting datasets include:

1. Gaining the ability to train and test the model on different types of data than the data used for training

2. Testing the model's accuracy, which is better than testing the accuracy of out-of-sample training

3. Ability to evaluate predictions using response values for the test datasets

They will then use the linear regression method from Python's sci-kit-learn library to create and train their model, which will try to imitate the function they created for the ML training dataset. At this point, they will need to determine whether their model can imitate the programmed function and generate the correct answer or accurate prediction.

Here, the ML model analyzes the training data and uses it to calculate the coefficients or weights to assign to the inputs to return the right outputs. By providing it with the right test data, the model will arrive at the correct answer.

Conditional or Decision Statements

In programming, we normally set certain conditions and decide which particular action to perform depending on the conditions. To do this, Python uses the "if statement" to check the program current state before responding suitably to that state. However, in this chapter, you will be exposed to various ways to write conditional statements. Furthermore, you will learn basic "if statements," create complex if statements and write loops to handle items in a list. There is so much more loaded in this chapter for you to learn. Without further ado, let us begin with a simple example.

The program below shows how you can use "if statement" to respond to a particular situation correctly. For instance, we have a list of colors and want to generate an output of different colors. Furthermore, the first letter should be in the title case of the lower case.

```
colors =["Green", "Blue", "Red", "Yellow"]
for color in colors:
print(color.title())
```

The output will be as follows:

```
Green
Blue
Red
Yellow
```

Consider another example where we want to print a list of cars. We have to print them in the title case since it is a proper name. Additionally, the value "Kia" must be in uppercase.

```
cars = ["Toyota," "Kia," "Audi," "Infinity"]
for car1 in cars:
if car1 == "kia":
print(car1.upper())
else:
print(car1.title())
```

The loop first verifies if whether the current value of the car is "Kia." If that is true, it then prints the value in uppercase. However, if it is not kia, it prints it in title case. The output will look like this:

```
Toyota
KIA
Audi
Infinity
```

The example above combines different concepts, which at the end of this chapter, you will learn. However, let us begin with the various conditional tests.

Conditional Tests in Python

The center of any if statement lies an expression, which must be evaluated to be either true or false. This is what is normally known as a conditional test because Python uses both values to determine if a particular code should be executed. If the particular statement is true, Python executes the code that follows it. However, if it is false, it ignores the code after it.

Checking Equality

At times, we may test for the equality of a particular condition. In this situation, we test if the value of the variable is equal to the other variable we decide. For instance:

```
>>> color = "green"
>>> color == "green"
True
```

In this example, we first assign the variable color with the value "green by using the single equal sign. This is not something new, as we have been using it throughout this book. However, the second line checks if the value of color is green, which has a double equal sign. It will return true if the value on the left side and that on the right side are both true. If it doesn't match, then the result will be false. When the value of the color is anything besides green, then this condition equates to false. The example below will clarify that.

```
>>> color = "green"
>>> color == "blue"
False
```

Note: When you test for equality, you should know that it is case sensitive. For instance, two values that have different capitalizations won't be regarded as equal. For instance,

```
>>>color = "Green"
>>> color == "green"
False
```

If the case is important, then this is advantageous. However, if the case of the variable isn't important, and you want to check the values, then you can convert the value of the variable to lowercase before checking for equality.

```
>>> color = "Green"
```

```
>>> color.lower() == "green"
True
```

This code will return True irrespective of how to format the value "Green" is because the conditional tests aren't case sensitive. Please note that the lower() function we used in the program does not change the value originally stored in color.

In the same way, we can check for equality; we can also check for inequality in a program code. In checking for inequality, we verify if two values are not equal and then return it as true. To check for inequality, Python has its unique symbol, which is a combination of the exclamation sign with an equal sign (!=). Most programming language uses these signs to represent inequality. The example below shows the use of if statement to test for inequality

```
color = "green"
if color != "blue"
print("The color doesn't match")
```

In the second line, the interpreter matches the value of color to that of "blue." If the values match, then Python return false; however, if it is true, Python returns true before executing the statement following it "The color doesn't match"

```
The color doesn't match
```

Numerical Comparison in Python

We can also test numerical values in Python, but it is very straightforward. For instance, the code below determines if a person's age is 25 years old:

```
>>>myage = 25
```

```
>>>myage == 25
True
```

Additionally, we can also test if two numbers are unequal. Consider the code below.

```
number = 34
if number != 54:
print("The number does not match. Please retry!")
```

The first line declares number as a variable and stores the number "34" in it. The conditional statement begins in line two and passes through the line because the number 34 is not equal to 54. Since the code is indented, the code is then executed to produce

```
The number does not match. Please retry!
```

Besides this, you can perform various mathematical comparison inside your conditional expressions including greater than, greater than or equal to , less than, and less than or equal to.

```
>>> number = 22
>>> number <25
True
>>> number <= 25
True
>>> number > 25
False
>>> number >= 25
 False
```

Every mathematical comparison you want can be included as part of an "if statement" that allows you to detect the particular condition in question.

Creating Multiple Conditions

When writing code, some situations may warrant you to verify multiple conditions simultaneously. For instance, you require conditions to be false to take action. At times, you may want only one condition to be satisfied. In this situation, you can use the keyword "or" and "and." Let first use the "and" keyword to check multiple conditions in Python programming.

Using "AND"

If you want to verify that two expressions are both true at the same time, the keyword "and" serves that purpose. The expression is evaluated to be true when both conditions test to return true. However, if one of the condition falls, then the expression returns false. For instance, you want to ascertain if two students in a class have over 45 score marks.

```
>>> score_1 = 46
>>> score_2 = 30
>>> score_1 >=45 and score_2 >= 45
False
>>> score_2 = 47
>>> score_1 >= 45 and score_2 >= 45
True
```

The program looks complicated but lets me explain it step-by-step. In the first two lines, we define two scores, score_1, and score_2. However, in line 3, we perform a check to ascertain if both scores are equal to or above 45. The condition on the right-hand side is false, but that of the left-hand side is true. Then in the line after the false statement, I changed the value of score_2 from 30 to 47. In this instant, the value of score_2 is now greater than 46; therefore, both conditions will evaluate to true.

To make the code more readable, we can use parentheses in each test. However, it is not compulsory to do such but makes it simpler. Let us use parentheses to demonstrate the difference between the previous code and the one below.

```
(score_1 >= 45) and (score_2 >=45)
```

Using "OR"

The "OR" keyword allows you to check multiple conditions as the "AND" keyword. However, the difference here is that the "OR" keyword is used when you want to ascertain that one expression is true for multiple conditions. In this situation, if one of the expression is false, the condition returns true. It returns false when both conditions are false.

Let us consider our previous example using the "OR" keyword. For instance, you want to ascertain if two students in a class have over 45 score mark.

```
>>> score_1 = 46
>>> score_2 = 30
>>> score_1 >=45 or score_2 >= 45
True
>>> score_1 = 30
>>> score_1 >= 45 or score_2 >= 45
False
```

We began by declaring two variables score_1 and score_2 and assign values to them. In the third line, we test the OR condition using the two variables. The test in that line satisfies the condition because one of the expressions is true. Then, it changed the value of the variable score to 30; however, it fails both conditions and therefore evaluates false.

Besides using the "And" and "OR" conditional statements to check multiple conditions, we can also test the availability of a value in a particular list. For instance, you want to verify if a username requested is already in existence from a list of usernames before the completion of online registration on a website.

To do this, we can use the "in" keyword in such a situation. For instance, let us use a list of animals in the zoo and check if it already on the list.

```
>>>animals = ["zebra", "lion", "crocodile", "monkey"]
>>> "monkey" in animals
True
>>> "rat" in animals
False
```

In the second and fourth lines, we use the "in" keyword to test if the request word in a double quote exists in our list of animals. The first test ascertains that "monkey" exists in our list, whereas the second test returns false because the rat is not in the animal's list. This method is significant because we can generate lists of important values and check the existence of the values in the list.

There are situations where you want to check if a value isn't in a list. In such a case, instead of using the "in" keyword to return false, we can use the "not" keyword. For instance, let us consider a list of Manchester United players before allowing them to be part of their next match. In order words, we want to scan the real players and ensure that the club does not field an illegible player.

```
united_player = ["Rashford," "Young," "Pogba," "Mata," "De Gea"]
```

```
player = "Messi"
if player not in united_player:
print(f "{player.title()}, you are not qualified to
play for Manchester United.")
```

The line "if player, not in united_player:" reads quite clearly. Peradventure, the value of the player isn't in the list united_player, Python returns the expression to be True and then executed the line indented under it. The player "Messi" isn't part of the list united_player; therefore, he will receive a message about his qualification status. The output will be as follow:

```
Messi, you are not qualified to play for Manchester United.
```

Boolean Expressions in Python

If you have learned any programming language, you might have come across the term "Boolean Expression" because they are very important. A Boolean expression is another term to describe the conditional test. When evaluated, the outcome can only be either True or False. However, they are essential if your goal is to keep track of specific conditions like if a user can change content or light is switched on or not. For instance,

```
change_content = False
light_on = False
light_off = True
```

Boolean values provide the best means of tracking the particular condition of a program.

Exercises to Try

Conditional Testing – Write various conditional expressions. Furthermore, print a statement to describe each condition and what the likely output of each test will be. for instance, your code can be like this:

```
car = "Toyota"
print("Is car == 'Toyota'? My prediction is True."(
print (car == "Toyota")
print("\nIs car == 'KIA'? My prediction is False.")
print(car== "KIA")
```

Test the following condition to evaluate either True or False using any things of your choice to form a list.

1. Test for both inequality and equality using strings and numbers

2. Test for the condition using the "or" and "and" keywords

3. Test if an item exists in the above list

4. Test if an item doesn't exist in the list.

If Statements

Since you now know conditional tests, it will be easier for you to under if statements. There are various types of if statements to use in Python, depending on your choice. In this section, you will learn the different if statements possible and the best situation to apply them, respectively.

Simple If Statements

In any programming language, the "if statement" is the simplest to come across. It only requires a test or condition with a single action following it, respectively. The syntax for this statement is as follows:

```
if condition:
perform action
```

The first line can contain any conditional statement with the second following the action to take. Ensure to indent the second line for clarity purposes. If the conditional statement is true, then the code under the condition is executed. However, if it is false, the code is ignored.

For instance, we have set a standard that the minimum score for a person to qualify for a football match is 20. We want to test if such a person is qualified to participate.

```
person = 21
if person >= 20
print("You are qualified for the football match against Valencia.")
```

In the first line, we define the person's age to 21 to qualify. Then the second line evaluates if the person is greater than or equal to 20. Python then executes the statement below because it fulfills the condition that the person is above 20.

```
You are qualified for the football match against Valencia.
```

Indentation is very significant when using the "if statement" like we did in the "for loop" situations. All indented lines are executed once the condition is satisfied after the if statement. However, if the statement returns false, then the whole code under it is ignored, and the program halted.

We can also include more code inside the if statements to display what we want. Let us add another line to display that the match is between Chelsea and Valencia at the Standford Bridge.

```
person  =21
if person >= 20
print("You are qualified for the football match against Valencia.")
print("The match is between Arsenal and Valencia.")
Print("The Venue is at the Emirate Stadium in England.")
```

The conditional statement passes through the condition and prints the indented actions once the condition is satisfied. The output will be as follow:

```
You are qualified for the football match against Valencia.
The match is between Arsenal and Valencia.
The Venue is at the Emirate Stadium in England.
```

Assuming the age is less than 20, and then there won't be any output for this program. let us try another example before going into another conditional statement.

```
name = "Abraham Lincoln"
if name = "Abraham Lincoln"
print("Abraham Lincoln was a great United State President.")
print("He is an icon that many presidents try to
```

emulate in the world.")

The output will be:

```
Abraham Lincoln was a great United State President.
He is an icon that many presidents try to emulate in
the world.
```

if-else Statements

At times, you may want to take certain actions if a particular condition isn't met. For example, you may decide what will happen if a person isn't qualified to play a match. Python provides the if-else statements to make this possible. The syntax is as follows:

```
if conditional test
perform statement_1
else
perform statement_2
```

Let us use our football match qualification to illustrate how to use the if-else statement.

```
person =18
if person >= 20:
print("You are qualified for the football match against Valencia.")
print("The match is between Arsenal and Valencia.")
Print("The Venue is at the Emirate Stadium in England.")
else:
print("Unfortunately, you are not qualified to participate in the match.")
print("Sorry, you have to wait until you are
```

qualified.")

The conditional test (if person>=20) is first evaluated to ascertain that the person is above 20 before it passes to the first indented line of code. If it is true, then it prints the statements beneath the condition. However, in our example, the conditional test will evaluate to false then passes control to the else section. Finally, it prints the statement below it since it fulfills that part of the condition.

```
Unfortunately, you are not qualified to participate in
the match.
Sorry, you have to wait until you are qualified.
```

This program works because of the two possible scenarios to evaluate – a person must be qualified to play or not play. In this situation, the if-else statement works perfectly when you want Python to execute one action in two possible situations.

Let us try another.

```
station_numbers = 10
if station_numbers >=12:
print("We need additional 3 stations in this
company.")
else:
print("We need additional 5 stations to meet the
demands of our audience.")
```

The output will be:

```
We need an additional 5 stations to meet the demands
of our audience.
```

The if-elif-else Chain

At times, you may want to test three different conditions based on certain criteria. In such a situation, Python allows us to use the if-elif-else conditional statement to execute such a task. We have many real-life situations require more than two possibilities. For instance, think of a cinema hall with different charge rates for different sets of people.

Children under 5 years are free

Children between 5 years and 17 years are $30

People older than 18 years is $50

As you can see, there are three possible situations because the following set of people can attend the cinema to watch the movie of their choice. In this situation, how can you ascertain a person's rate? Well, the following code will illustrate that point and print out specific price rates for each category of people.

```
person_age = 13
if person_age < 5:
print("Your ticket cost is $0.")
elif person_age < 17:
print("Your ticket cost is $30.")
else:
print("Your ticket cost is $50)
```

The first line declares a variable "person_age" with value 13. Then we perform the first conditional statement to test if the person is below the age of 5. If it fulfills the condition, it prints the appropriate message, and the program halts. However, if it returns false, it passes to the elif line, which tests if the person_age is less than 17. At this post, the person's minimum age must be 5 years and not above 17. If the person is above 17, then Python skips the instruction and goes to the next condition.

In the example, we fix the person_age to 13. Therefore, the first test will evaluate false and won't execute the block of line. It then tests the elif condition, which in this case is true, and will print the message. The output will be:

```
Your ticket cost is $30.")
```

Nevertheless, if the age is above 17, then it will pass through the first two tests because it will evaluate to false. Then the next command will be the else condition, which will print the statement below.

We can rewrite this program in such a way that we won't have to include the message "Your ticket cost is..". all we need is to put the prince inside the if-elif-else chain with a simple print() method to execute after the evaluation of the chain. Look at the line of code below:

```
person_age = 13
if person_age < 5:
cost = 0
elif person_age < 17:
cost =30
else:
cost = 50
print(f "Your ticket cost is ${cost}.")
```

In the third, fifth, and seventh lines, we defined the cost based on the person's age. The cost price is already set within the if-elif-else statement. However, the last line uses the cost of each age to form the final cost of the ticket.

This new code will produce the same result as the previous example. However, the latter is more concise and straightforward. Instead of using three different print statement, our reverse code only use a single print statement to print the cost of the ticket.

Multiple elif Blocks

You can also have more than one elif block in your program. For instance, if the manager of the cinema decides to implement special discounts for workers, this will require additional, conditional tests to the program to ascertain whether the person in question is qualified for such a discount. Assuming those above 55 years will pay 70% of the initial cost of each ticket. Then the program code will be as follows:

```
person_age = 13
if person_age < 5:
cost = 0
elif person_age < 17:
cost =30
elif person_age < 55
cost = 50
else:
cost = 35
print(f "Your ticket cost is ${cost}.")
```

The cost is identical to our previous example; however, the only including is the "elif person_age < 55" and is respective else condition. This second elif block checks if the person's age is less than 55 before assigning them the cost of the ticket for $50. However, the statement after the else needs to be changed. In this situation, it is applicable if the person's age is above 55 years, which is this situation fulfills the condition we want.

The "else" statement isn't compulsory because you can omit it and use the elif statement instead. At times, it is better to use additional elif statements to capture specific interests. Let us see how to implement it without using the else statement.

```
person_age = 13
if person_age < 5:
cost = 0
elif person_age < 17:
cost =30
elif person_age < 55:
cost = 50
elif person_age >= 55:
cost = 35
print(f "Your ticket cost is ${cost}.")
```

The additional elif statement helps to assign the ticket cost of "$30" to those above 30 years. This format is a bit clearer when compared with the else block.

Performing Multiple Conditions

Using the if-elif-else statement comes handy when especially when you want to pass only one test. Once the interpreter discovers that this test is passed, it skips other tests and halts the program. With this feature, you test a specific condition in a line of code.

Nevertheless, some situations may warrant you to check all the conditions available. In such a scenario, you can use multiple if statements without adding the elif or else blocks. This method becomes relevant when more than one of the condition returns true.

For instance, let us consider the previous example of players in Manchester United to illustrate this. In this, we want to include the players in an upcoming match against their rivals Manchester City.

```
united_players = ["Rashford," "Young," "Pogba," "Mata," "De Gea"]
if "Young" in united_players:
print("Adding Young to the team list.")
if "De Gea" in united_players:
print("Adding Dea Gea to the team list.")
if "Messi" in united_players:
print("Adding Messi to the team list.")
print( "\ Team list completed for the match against Manchester City!")
```

In the first line, we defined united_players as a variable with values Rashford, Young, Pogba, Mata, and De Gea. The second line uses the "if statement" to check if the person requested for Young. The same applies to the lines with the "if statement" and the condition is run regardless of the outcome of the previous tests. For this program above, the output will be:

```
Adding Young to the team list.
Adding Dea Gea to the team list.
Team list completed for the match against Manchester City!
```

If we decide to use the if-elif-else block, the code won't function properly because once a particular test returns true, the program will stop. Let us try it and see.

```
united_players = ["Rashford," "Young," "Pogba," "Mata," "De Gea"]
if "Young" in united_players:
print("Adding Young to the team list.")
```

```
elif  "De Gea" in united_players:
print("Adding Dea Gea to the team list.")
elif  "Messi" in united_players:
print("Adding Messi to the team list.")
print( "\ Team list completed for the match against Manchester City!")
```

In this code, Python will evaluate the first condition, and once it is true, the program stops. The output for this program will be:

```
Adding Young to the team list.
Team list completed for the match against Manchester City!
```

Exercise to Try

Consider the list of colors we have in the world. Create a variable name color and assign the following colors to it – blue, red, black, orange, white, yellow, indigo, green.

Use an "if statement" to check if the color is blue. If the color is blue, then print a message indicating a score of 5 points.

Write a problem using the if-else chain to print if a particular selected is green.

Write another program using the if-elif-else chain to determine the scores of students in a class. Set a variable "score" to store the student's score.

If the student's score is below 40, indicate an output a message that such student has failed

If the student's score is above 41 but less than 55, print a message that the student has passed.

Essential Libraries for Machine Learning in Python

Many developers nowadays prefer the usage of Python in their data analysis. Python is not only applied in data analysis but also statistical techniques. Scientists, especially the ones dealing with data, also prefer using Python in data integration. That's the integration of Webb apps and other environment productions.

The features of Python have helped scientists to use it in Machine Learning. Examples of these qualities include consistent syntax, being flexible and even having a shorter time in development. It also can develop sophisticated models and has engines that could help in predictions.

As a result, Python boasts of having a series or set of very extensive libraries. Remember, libraries refer to a series of routines and sorts of functions with different languages. Therefore, a robust library can lead to tackling more complex tasks. However, this is possible without writing several code lines again. It is good to note that Machine Learning relies majorly on mathematics. That's mathematical optimization, elements of probability and also statistical data. Therefore, Python comes in with a rich knowledge of performing complex tasks without much involvement.

The following are examples of essential libraries being used in our present.

Scikit – Learn

Scikit learn is one of the best and a trendy library in Machine

Learning. It has the ability to supporting learning algorithms, especially unsupervised and supervised ones.

Examples of Scikit learn include the following.
- *k-means*
- decision trees
- linear and logistic regression
- *clustering*

This kind of library has major components from NumPy and SciPy. Scikit learn has the power to add algorithms sets that are useful in Machine Learning and also tasks related to data mining. That's, it helps in classification, clustering, and even regression analysis. There are also other tasks that this library can efficiently deliver. A good example includes ensemble methods, feature selection, and more so, data transformation. It is good to understand that the pioneers or experts can easily apply this if at all, they can be able to implement the complex and sophisticated parts of the algorithms.

TensorFlow

It is a form of algorithm which involves deep learning. They are not always necessary, but one good thing about them is their ability to give out correct results when done right. It will also enable you to run your data in a CPU or GPU. That's, you can write data in the Python program, compile it then run it on your central processing unit. Therefore, this gives you an easy time in performing your analysis. Again, there is no need for having these pieces of information written at C++ or instead of other levels such as CUDA.

TensorFlow uses nodes, especially the multi-layered ones. The nodes perform several tasks within the system, which include employing networks such as artificial neutral, training, and even set up a high volume of datasets. Several search engines such as Google depend on this type of library. One main application of this is the identification of objects. Again, it helps in different Apps that deal with the recognition of voice.

Theano

Theano too forms a significant part of Python library. Its vital tasks here are to help with anything related to numerical computation. We can also relate it to NumPy. It plays other roles such as;

- Definition of mathematical expressions
- Assists in the optimization of mathematical calculation
- Promotes the evaluation of expressions related to numerical analysis.

The main objective of Theano is to give out efficient results. It is a faster Python library as it can perform calculations of intensive data up to 100 times. Therefore, it is good to note that Theano works best with GPU as compared to the CPU of a computer. In most industries, the CEO and other personnel use Theano for deep learning. Also, they use it for computing complex and sophisticated tasks. All these became possible due to its processing speed. Due to the expansion of industries with a high demand for data computation techniques, many people are opting for the latest version of this library. Remember, the latest one came to limelight some years back. The new version of Theano, that's, version 1.0.0, had several improvements, interface changes and composed of new features.

Pandas

Pandas is a library that is very popular and helps in the provision of data structures that are of high level and quality. The data provided here is simple and easy to use. Again, it's intuitive. It is composed of various sophisticated inbuilt methods which make it capable of performing tasks such as grouping and timing analysis. Another function is that it helps in a combination of data and also offering filtering options. Pandas can collect data from other sources such as Excel, CSV, and even SQL databases. It also can manipulate the collected data to undertake its operational roles within the industries. Pandas consist of two structures that enable it to perform its functions correctly. That's Series which has only one dimensional and data frames that boast of two dimensional. Pandas has been regarded as the most strong and powerful Python library over the time being. Its main function is to help in data manipulation. Also, it has the power to export or import a wide range of data. It is applicable in various sectors, such as in the field of Data Science.

Pandas is effective in the following areas:

- Splitting of data
- Merging of two or more types of data
- Data aggregation
- Selecting or subsetting data
- Data reshaping

Diagrammatic explanations

Series Dimensional

A	7
B	8

C	9
D	3
E	6
F	9

Data Frames dimensional

	A	B	C	D
*0	0	0	0	0
*1	7	8	9	3
*2	14	16	18	6
*3	21	24	27	9
*4	28	32	36	12
*5	35	40	45	15

Applications of pandas in a real-life situation will enable you to perform the following:
- You can quickly delete some columns or even add some texts found within the Dataframe
- It will help you in data conversion
- Pandas can reassure you of getting the misplaced or missing data
- It has a powerful ability, especially in the grouping of other programs according to their functionality.

Matplotlib

This is another sophisticated and helpful data analysis technique that helps in data visualization. Its main objective is to advise the industry where it stands using the various inputs. You will realize that your production goals are meaningless when you fail to share them with different stakeholders. To perform this, Matplotlib comes in handy with the types of computation analysis required. Therefore, it is the only Python library that every scientist, especially the ones dealing with data prefers. This type of library has good looks when it comes to graphics and images. More so, many prefer using it in creating various graphs for data analysis. However, the technological world has completely changed with new advanced libraries flooding the industry.

It is also flexible, and due to this, you are capable of making several graphs that you may need. It only requires a few commands to perform this.

In this Python library, you can create various diverse graphs, charts of all kinds, several histograms, and even scatterplots. You can also make non-Cartesian charts too using the same principle.

Diagrammatic explanations

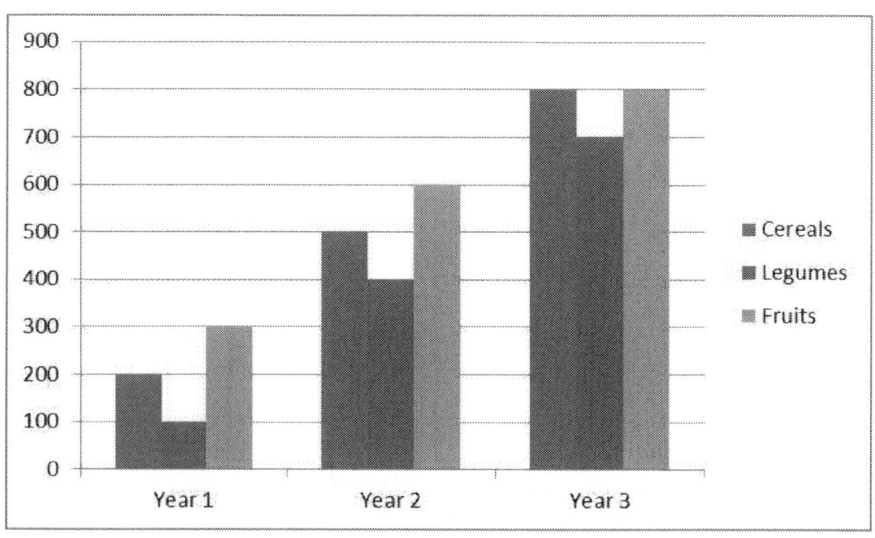

The above graph highlights the overall production of a company within three years. It specifically demonstrates the usage of Matplotlib in data analysis. By looking at the diagram, you will realize that the production was high as compared to the other two years. Again, the company tends to perform in the production of fruits since it was leading in both years 1 and 2 with a tie in year 3. From the figure, you realize that your work of presentation, representation and even analysis has been made easier as a result of using this library. This Python library will eventually enable you to come up with good graphics images, accurate data and much more. With the help of this Python library, you will be able to note down the year your production was high, thus, being in a position to maintain the high productivity season.

It is good to note that this library can export graphics and can change these graphics into PDF, GIF, and so on. In summary, the following tasks can be undertaken with much ease. They include:

- Formation of line plots
- Scattering of plots
- Creations of beautiful bar charts and building up of histograms
- Application of various pie charts within the industry
- Stemming the schemes for data analysis and computations
- Being able to follow up contours plots
- Usage of spectrograms
- Quiver plots creation

Seaborn

Seaborn is also among the popular libraries within the Python category. Its main objective here is to help in visualization. It is important to note that this library borrows its foundation from

Matplotlib. Due to its higher level, it is capable of various plots generation such as the production of heat maps, processing of violin plots and also helping in generation of time series plots.

Diagrammatic Illustrations

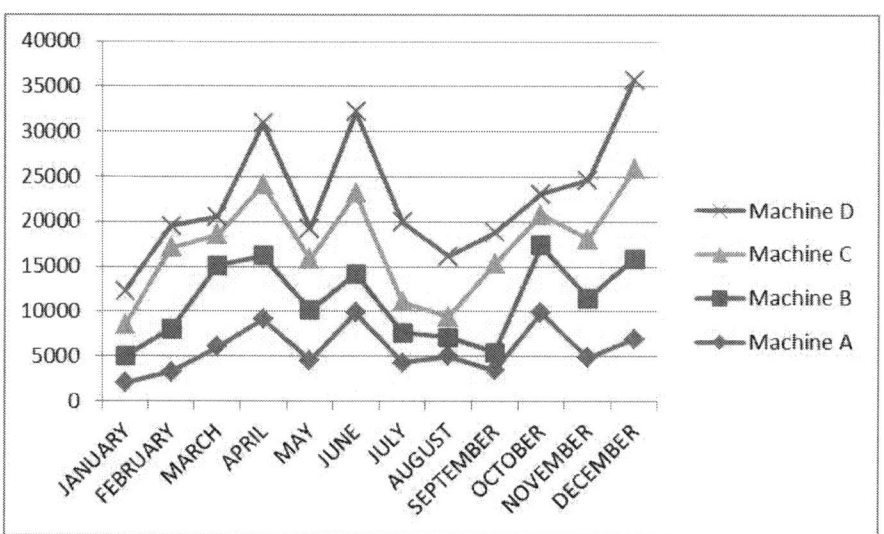

The above line graph clearly shows the performance of different machines the company is using. Following the diagram above, you can eventually deduce and make a conclusion on which machines the company can keep using to get the maximum yield. On most occasions, this evaluation method by the help of the Seaborn library will enable you to predict the exact abilities of your different inputs. Again, this information can help for future reference in the case of purchasing more machines. Seaborn library also has the power to detect the performance of other variable inputs within the company.

For example, the number of workers within the company can be easily identified with their corresponding working rate.

NumPy

This is a very widely used Python library. Its features enable it to perform multidimensional array processing. Also, it helps in the matrix processing. However, these are only possible with the help of an extensive collection of mathematical functions. It is important to note that this Python library is highly useful in solving the most significant computations within the scientific sector. Again, NumPy is also applicable in areas such as linear algebra, derivation of random number abilities used within industries and more so Fourier transformation. NumPy is also used by other high-end Python libraries such as TensorFlow for Tensors manipulation. In short, NumPy is mainly for calculations and data storage. You can also export or load data to Python since it has those features that enable it to perform these functions. It is also good to note that this Python library is also known as numerical Python.

SciPy

This is among the most popular library used in our industries today. It boasts of comprising of different modules that are applicable in the optimization sector of data analysis. It also plays a significant role in integration, linear algebra, and other forms of mathematical statistics.

In many cases, it plays a vital role in image manipulation. Manipulation of the image is a process that is widely applicable in day to day activities. Cases of Photoshops and much more are examples of SciPy. Again, many organizations prefer SciPy in their image manipulation, especially the pictures used for presentation. For instance, wildlife society can come up with the description of a cat and then manipulate it using different colors to suit their project. Below is an example that can help you understand this more straightforwardly. The picture has been manipulated:

The original input image was a cat that the wildlife society took. After manipulation and resizing the image according to our preferences, we get a tinted image of a cat.

Keras

This is also part and parcel of Python library, especially within Machine Learning. It belongs to the group of networks with high level neural. It is significant to note that Keras has the capability of working over other libraries, especially TensorFlow and even Theano. Also, it can operate nonstop without mechanical failure. In addition to this, it seems to work better on both the GPU and CPU. For most beginners in Python programming, Keras offers a secure pathway towards their ultimate understanding. They will be in a position to design the network and even to build it. Its ability to prototype faster and more quickly makes it the best Python library among the learners.

PyTorch

This is another accessible but open source kind of Python library. As a result of its name, it boasts of having extensive choices when it comes to tools. It is also applicable in areas where we have computer vision. Computer vision and visual display play an essential role in several types of research. Again, it aids in the processing of Natural Language. More so, PyTorch can undertake some technical tasks that are for developers. That's enormous calculations and data analysis using computations. It can also help in graph creation which mainly used for computational purposes. Since it is an open-source Python library, it can work or perform tasks on other libraries such as Tensors. In combination with Tensors GPU, its acceleration will increase.

Scrapy

Scrapy is another library used for creating crawling programs. That's spider bots and much more. The spider bots frequently help in data retrieval purposes and also applicable in the formation of URLs used on the web. From the beginning, it was to assist in data scrapping. However, this has undergone several evolutions and led to the expansions of its general purpose. Therefore, the main task of the scrappy library in our present-day is to act as crawlers for general use. The library led to the promotion of general usage, application of universal codes, and so on.

Statsmodels

Statsmodels is a library with the aim of data exploration using several methods of statistical computations and data assertions. It has many features such as result statistics and even characteristic features. It can undertake this role with the help of the various models such as linear regression, multiple estimators, and analysis involving time series, and even using more linear models. Also, other models, such as discrete choice are applicable here.

What is the TensorFlow Library

The next thing that we need to spend some time looking at is the TensorFlow Library. This is another option that comes from Python, and it can help you to get some Machine Learning done. This one takes on a few different options of what you can do when it comes to Machine Learning, so it is definitely worth your time to learn how to use this option along with the algorithms that we talked about with the Scikit-Learn library.

TensorFlow is another framework that you can work with in Python Machine Learning, and it is going to offer the programmer a few different features and tools to get your project done compared to the others. You will find that the framework that comes with TensorFlow is going to come from Google, and it is helpful when you are trying to work on some models that are deep learning related. TensorFlow is going to rely on graphs of data flow for numerical computation. And it can make sure that some of the different things that you can do with Machine Learning are easier than ever before.

TensorFlow is going to help us out in many different ways. First, it can help us with acquiring the data, training the models of Machine Learning that we are trying to use, helps to make predictions, and can even modify a few of the future results that we have to make them work more efficiently. Since each of these steps is going to be important when it comes to doing some Machine Learning, we can see how TensorFlow can come into our project and ensure we reach that completion that we want even better.

First, let's take a look at what TensorFlow is all about and some of the background that comes with this Python library. The Brain team from Google was the first to develop TensorFlow to use on large scale options of Machine Learning. It was developed in order to bring together different algorithms for both deep learning and

Machine Learning, and it is going to make them more useful through what is known as a common metaphor. TensorFlow works along with the Python language that we talked about before. In addition to this, it is going to provide the users with a front-end API that is easy to use when working on a variety of building applications.

It makes it a bit further, though. Even though you can work with TensorFlow and it matches up with the Python coding language while you do the coding and the algorithms, it is going to be able to change these up. All of the applications that you use with the help of TensorFlow are going to be executed using the C++ language instead, giving them an even higher level of performance than before.

TensorFlow can be used for a lot of different actions that you would need to do to make a Machine Learning project a success. Some of the things that you can do with this library, in particular, will include running, training, and building up the deep neural networks, doing some image recognition, working with recurrent neural networks, digit classification, natural language processing, and even word embedding. And this is just a few of the things that are available for a programmer to do when they work with TensorFlow with Machine Learning.

Installing TensorFlow

With this in mind, we need to take some time to learn how to install TensorFlow on a computer before we can use this library. Just like we did with Scikit-Learn, we need to go through and set up the environment and everything else so that this library is going to work. You will enjoy that with this kind of library; it is already going to be set up with a few APIs for programming (we will take a look at these in more depth later on), including Rust, Go, C++ and Java to name a few. We are going to spend our time here looking at the way that the TensorFlow library is going to work on the Windows system, but the steps that you have to use to add this library to your other operating systems are going to be pretty much the same.

Now, when you are ready to set up and download the TensorFlow library on your Windows computer, you will be able to go through two choices on how to download this particular library. You can choose either to work with the Anaconda program to get it done, or a pip is going to work well, too. The native pip is helpful because it takes all of the parts that go with the TensorFlow library and will make sure that it is installed on your system. And you get the bonus of the system doing this for you without needing to have a virtual environment set up to get it done.

However, this one may seem like the best choice, but it can come with some problems along the way. Installing the TensorFlow library using a pip can be a bit faster and doesn't require that virtual environment, but it can come with some interference to the other things that you are doing with Python. Depending on what you plan to do with Python, this can be a problem so consider that before starting.

The good thing to remember here is that if you do choose to work with a pip and it doesn't seem like it is going to interfere with what you are doing too much, you will be able to get the whole TensorFlow library to run with just one single command. And once you are done with this command, the whole library, and all of the parts that you need with it, are going to be set up and ready to use on the computer with just one command. And the pip even makes it easier for you to choose the directory that you would like to use to store the TensorFlow library for easier use.

In addition to using the pip to help download and install the TensorFlow library, it is also possible for you to use the Anaconda program. This one is going to take a few more commands to get started, but it does prevent any interference from happening with the Python program, and it allows you to create a virtual environment that you can work with and test out without a ton of interference or other issues with what is on your computer.

Though there are a few benefits to using the Anaconda program instead of a pip, it is often recommended that you install this program right along with a pip, rather than working with just the conda install. With this in mind, we will still show you some of the steps that it takes to just use the conda install on its own so you can do this if you choose.

One more thing that we need to consider here before moving on is that you need to double-check which version of Python is working. Your version needs to be at Python 3.5 or higher for this to work for you. Python 3 uses the pip 3 program, and it is the best and most compatible when it comes to working with a TensorFlow install. Working with an older version is not going to work as well with this library and can cause some issues when you try to do some of your Machine Learning code.

You can work with either the CPU or the GPU version of this library based on what you are the most comfortable with. The first code below is the CPU version and the second code below is going to be the GPU version.

```
pip 3 install - upgrade tensorflow
pip 3 install - upgrade tensorflow-gpu
```

Both of these commands are going to be helpful because they are going to ensure that the TensorFlow library is going to be installed on your Windows system. But another option that you can use is with the Anaconda package itself. The methods above were still working with the pip installs, but we talked about how there are a few drawbacks when it comes to this one.

Pip is the program that is already installed automatically when you install Python onto your system as well. But you may find out quickly that Anaconda is not. This means that if you want to ensure that you can get TensorFlow to install with this, then you need to first install the Anaconda program. To do this, just go to the website for Anaconda and then follow the instructions that come up to help you get it done.

Once you have had the time to install the Anaconda program, then you will notice that within the files there is going to be a package that is known as conda. This is a good package to explore a bit at this time because it is going to be the part that helps you manage the installation packages, and it is helpful when it is time to manage the virtual environment. To help you get the access that you need with this package, you can just start up Anaconda and it will be there.

When Anaconda is open, you can go to the main screen on Windows, click the Start button, and then choose All programs from here. You need to go through and expand things out to look inside of Anaconda at the files that are there. You can then click on the prompt that is there for Anaconda and then get that to launch on your screen. If you wish to, it is possible to see the details of this package by opening the command line and writing in "conda info". This allows you to see some more of the details that you need about the package and the package manager.

The virtual environment that we talk about with the Anaconda program is going to be pretty simple to use, and it is pretty much just an isolated copy of Python. It will come with all of the capabilities that you need to maintain all of the files that you use, along with the directories and the paths that go with it too. This is going to be helpful because it allows you to do all of your coding inside the Python program, and allows you to add in some different libraries that are associated with Python if you choose.

These virtual environments may take a bit of time to adjust to and get used to, but they are good for working on Machine Learning because they allow you to isolate a project, and can help you to do some coding, without all of the potential problems that come with dependencies and version requirements. Everything you do in the virtual environment is going to be on its own, so you can experiment and see what works and what doesn't, without messing up other parts of the code.

From here, our goal is to take the Anaconda program and get it to work on creating the virtual environment that we want so that the package from TensorFlow is going to work properly. The conda command is going to come into play here again to make this happen. Since we are going through the steps that are needed to create a brand new environment now, we will need to name it tensorenviron, and then the rest of the syntax to help us get this new environment created includes:

```
conda create -n tensorenvrion
```

After you type this code into the compiler, the program is going to stop and ask you whether you want to create the new environment, or if you would rather cancel the work that you are currently doing. This is where we are going to type in the "y" key and then hit enter so that the environment is created. The installation may take a few minutes as the compiler completes the environment for you.

Once the new environment is created, you have to go through the process of actually activating it. Without this activation in place, you will not have the environment ready to go for you. You just need to use the command of "activate" to start and then list out the name of any environment that you want to work with to activate. Since we used the name of tensorenviron earlier, you will want to use this in your code as well. An example of how this is going to look includes:

Activate tensorenviron

Now that you have been able to activate the TensorFlow environment, it is time to go ahead and make sure that the package for TensorFlow is going to be installed too. You can do this by using the command below:

```
conda install tensorflow
```

When you get to this point, you will be presented with a list of all the packages that are available to install in case you want to add in a few others along with TensorFlow. You can then decide if you want to install one or more of these packages, or if you want to just stick with TensorFlow for right now. Make sure to agree that you want to do this and continue through the process.

The installation of this library is going to get to work right away. But it is going to be a process that takes some time so just let it go without trying to backspace or restart. The speed of your internet is going to make a big determinant of whether you will see this take a long time or not.

Soon though, the installation process for this library is going to be all done, and you can then go through and see if this installation process was successful or if you need to fix some things. The good news is the checking phase is going to be easy to work with because you can just use the import statement of Python to set it up.

This statement that we are writing is then going to go through the regular terminal that we have with Python. If you are still working here, like you should, with the prompt from Anaconda, then you would be able to hit enter after typing in the word Python. This will make sure that you are inside the terminal that you need for Python so you can get started. Once you are in the right terminal for this, type in the code below to help us get this done and make sure that TensorFlow is imported and ready to go:

```
import tensorflow as tf
```

At this point, the program should be on your computer and ready to go and we can move on to the rest of the guidebook and see some of the neat things that you can do with this library. There may be a chance that the TensorFlow package didn't end up going through the way that it should. If this is true for you, then the compiler is going to present you with an error message for you to read through and you need to go back and make sure the code has been written in the right format along the way.

The good news is if you finish doing this line of code above and you don't get an error message at all, then this means that you have set up the TensorFlow package the right way and it is ready to use! With that said, we need to explore some more options and algorithms that a programmer can do when it comes to using the TensorFlow library and getting to learn how they work with the different Machine Learning projects you want to implement.

Artificial Neural Networks

This chapter discusses the integral aspect of artificial neural networks. It also covers their component in particular activation functions and how to train an artificial neural network, as well as the different advantages of using an artificial neural network.

Definition of artificial neural network

The employment of artificial neural networks is a widely used approach in Machine Learning. It is inspired by the brain system of humans. The objective of neural networks is to replicate how the human brain learns. The neural network system is an ensemble of input and output layers and a hidden layer that transforms the input layer into useful information to the output layer. Usually, several hidden layers are implemented in an artificial neural network. The figure below presents an example of a neural network system composed of 2 hidden layers:

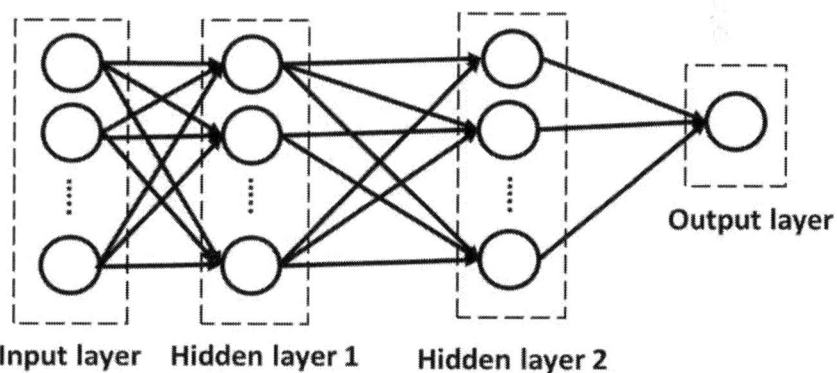

Example of an artificial neural network

Before going further and explaining how neural networks work, let's first define what a neuron is. A neuron is simply a mathematical equation expressed as the sum of the weighted inputs. Let's consider $X = \{x_1, x_2, \ldots, x_M\}$ a vector of M inputs, the neuron is a linear combination of all inputs defined as follows:

$$F(X = \{x_1, x_2, \ldots, x_M\}) = w_1 x_1 + w_2 x_2 + \ldots + w_M x_M,$$

being $w_1, w_2, \ldots, w_M$ the weights assigned to each input. The function F can also be represented as:

$$F(X) = WX$$

Where W is a weight matrix and X a vector of data. The second formulation is very convenient when programming a neural network model. The weights are determined during the training procedure. Training an artificial neural network means finding the optimal weights W that provide the most accurate output.

To each neuron, an activation function is applied the resulted weighted sum of inputs X. The role of the activation function is deciding whether the neuron should be activated or not according to the model's prediction. This process is applied to each layer of the network. In the next sub-sections, we will discuss in detail the role and types of activation functions as well as the different types of neural networks.

What is an activation function and its role in neural network models?

Activation functions are formulated as mathematical functions. These functions are a crucial component of an artificial neural network model. For each neuron, an activation function is associated. The activation function decides whether to activate the neuron or not. For instance, let's consider the output from a neuron, which is:

$$Y = \sum weight \times input + bias$$

The output Y can be of any value. The neuron does not have any information on the reasonable range of values that Y can take. For this purpose, the activation function is implemented in the neural network to check Y values and make a decision on whether the neural connections should consider this neuron activated or not.

There are different types of activation functions. The most instinctive function is the *step function*. This function sets a threshold and decides to activate or not activate a neuron if it exceeds a certain threshold. In other words, the output of this function is 1 if Y is greater than a threshold and 0 otherwise. Formally, the activation function is:

$$F = \begin{cases} 1, & if\ Y > threshold \\ 0, & otherwise \end{cases}$$

where 1 means 'activated' and 0 means 'not-activated'.

This activation function can be used for a classification problem where the output should be yes or no (i.e., 1 or 0). However, it has some drawbacks. For example, let's consider a set of several categories (i.e., class1, class2, ..., etc.) to which input may belong to.

If this activation function is used and more than one neuron is activated, the output will be 1 for all neurons. In this case, it is hard to distinguish between the classes and decide into which class the input belongs to because all neuron outputs are 1. In short, the step function does not support multiple output values and classification into several classes.

Linear activation function, unlike the step function, provides a range of activation values. It computes an output that is proportional to the input. Formally:

$$F(X) = WX,$$

where X is the input.

This function supports several outputs rather than just 1 or 0 values. This function, because it is linear, does not support backpropagation for model training. Backpropagation is the process that relies on function derivative or gradient to update the parameters, in particular, the weights. The derivative (i.e., gradient) of the linear activation function is a constant which is equal to W and is not related to changes in the input X. Therefore, it does not provide information on which weights applied to the input can give accurate predictions.

Moreover, all layers can be reduced to one layer when using the linear function. The fact that all layers are using a linear function, the final layer is a linear function of the first layer. So, no matter how many layers are used in the neural network, they are equivalent to the first layer, and there is no point in using multiple layers. A neural network with multiple layers connected with a linear activation function is just a linear regression model that cannot support the complexity of input data.

The majority of neural networks use non-linear activation functions because, in the majority of real-world applications, relations between the output and the input features are non-linear. The non-linear functions allow the neural network to map complex patterns between the inputs and the outputs. They also allow the neural network to learn the complex process that governs complex data or high dimension data such as images, audios, among others. The non-linear functions allow overcoming the drawbacks of linear functions and step functions. They support backpropagation (i.e., the derivative is not a constant and depends on the changes of the input) and stacking several layers (i.e., the combination of non-linear functions is non-linear). Several non-linear functions exist and can be used within a neural network. In this book, we are going to cover the most commonly used non-linear activation functions in Machine Learning applications.

The sigmoid function

The *sigmoid function* is one of the most used activation functions within an artificial neural network. Formally, a sigmoid function is equal to the inverse of the sum of 1 and the exponential of inputs:

$$F(X) = \frac{1}{1 + \exp(-X)}$$

Outputs of a sigmoid function are bounded by 0 and 1. More precisely, the outputs take any value between 0 and 1 and provide clear predictions. In fact, when the X is greater than 2 or lower than -2, the value of Y is close to the edge of the curve (i.e., closer to 0 or 1).

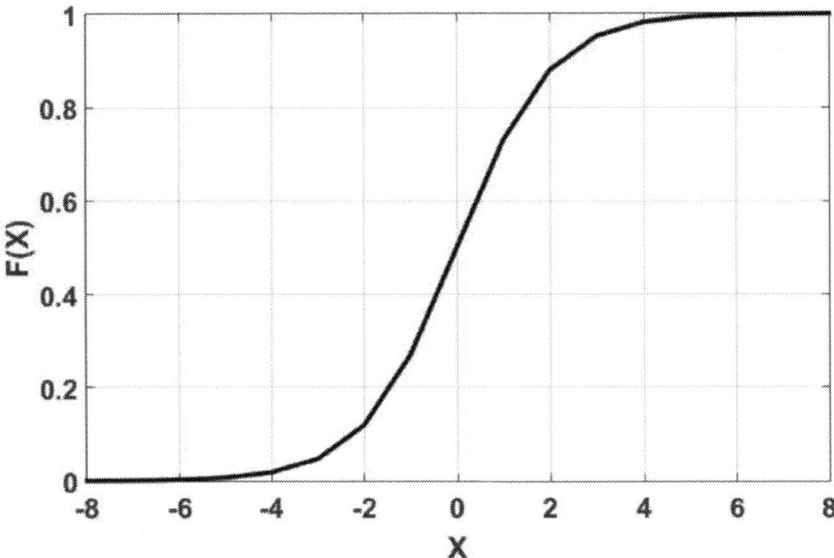

The disadvantage of this activation function, as we can see from the figure above, is the small change in the output for input values under -4 and above 4. This problem is called *'vanishing gradient'* which means that the gradient is very small on horizontal extremes of the curve. This makes a neural network using the sigmoid function, learning very slowly when they approach the edges and computationally expensive.

The tanh function

The *tanh function* is another activation function used that is similar to the sigmoid function. The mathematical formulation of this function is:

$$F(X) = \tanh(X) = \frac{2}{1 + \exp(-2X)} - 1$$

This function is a scaled sigmoid function. Therefore, it has the same characteristics as the sigmoid function. However, the outputs of this function range between -1 and 1, and the gradient are more pronounced than the gradient of the sigmoid function. Unlike the sigmoid function, the tanh function is zero-centered, which makes it very useful for inputs with negative, neutral, and positive values. The drawback of this function, as for the sigmoid function, is the vanishing gradient issue and computationally expensive.

The ReLu function

The *Rectified Linear Unit function* or what is known as *ReLu function,* is also a widely used activation function, which is computationally efficient. This function is efficient and allows the neural network to converge quickly compared to the sigmoid and tanh function because it uses simple mathematical formulations. ReLu returns X as output if X is positive or 0 otherwise. Formally, this activation function is formulated as

$$F(X) = \max(0, X)$$

This activation function is not bounded and takes values from 0 to +inf. Although it has a similar shape as a linear function (i.e., this function is equal to identity for positive values), the ReLu function has a derivative. The drawback of the ReLu is that the derivative (i.e., the gradient) is 0 when the inputs are negative. This means as for the linear functions, the backpropagation cannot be processed, and the neural network cannot learn unless the inputs are greater than 0. This aspect of the ReLu, gradient equal to 0 when the inputs are negative, is called the dying ReLu problem.

To prevent the dying ReLu problem, two ReLu variations can be used, namely the *Leaky ReLu function* and the *Parametric ReLu function*. The Leakey ReLu function returns as output the maximum of X and X by 0.1. In other words, the leaky ReLu is equal to the identity function when X is greater than 0 and is equal to the product of 0.1 and X when X is less than zero. This function is provided as follows:

$$F(X) = \max(0.1X, X)$$

This function has a small positive gradient which is 0.1 when X has negative values, which make this function support backpropagation for negative values. However, it may not provide a consistent prediction for these negative values.

The parametric ReLu function is similar to the Leaky ReLu function, which takes the gradient as a parameter to the neural network to define the output when X is negative. The mathematical formulation of this function is as follows:

$$F(X) = \max(aX, X)$$

There are other variations of the ReLu function such as the *exponential linear ReLu*. This function, unlike the other variations of the ReLu the Leaky ReLu and parametric ReLu, has a log curve for negative values of X instead of the linear curves like the Leaky ReLu and the parametric ReLu functions. The downside of this function is it saturates for large negative values of X. Other variations exist which all rely on the same concept of defining a gradient greater than 0 when X has negative values.

The Softmax function

The *Softmax function* is another type of activation function used differently than the one presented previously. This function is usually applied only to the output layer when a classification of the inputs into several different classes is needed. In fact, the Softmax function supports several classes and provides the probability of input to belong to a specific class. It normalizes outputs of every category between 0 and 1 then divides by their sum to provide that probability.

Given all these activation functions, where each one has its pros and cons, the question now is: which one should be used in a neural network? The answer is: simply having a better understanding of the problem in hand will help guide into a specific activation function, especially if the characteristics of the function being approximated are known beforehand. For instance, a sigmoid function is a good choice for a classification problem. In case the nature of the function being approximated is unknown, it is highly recommended to start with a ReLu function rather than trying other activation functions. Overall, the ReLu function works well for a wide range of applications. It is an ongoing research, and you may try your activation function.

An important aspect of choosing an activation function is the sparsity of the activation. Sparsity means that not all neurons are activated. This is a desired characteristic in a neural network because it makes the network learns faster and less prone to overfitting. Let's imagine a large neural network with multiple neurons if all neurons were activated; it means all these neurons are processed to describe the final output. This makes the neural network very dense and computationally exhaustive to process. The sigmoid and the tanh activation functions have this property of activating almost all neurons, which makes them computationally inefficient unlike the ReLu function and its variations that cause the inactivation of some negative values. That is the reason why it is recommended to start with the ReLu function when approximating a function with unknown characteristics.

What are the types of artificial neural networks?

Several categories of artificial neural networks with different properties and complexities exist. The first and simplest neural network developed is the perceptron. The *perceptron* computes the sum of the inputs, applies an activation function, and provides the result to the output layer.

Another old and simple approach is the *feedforward neural network*. This type of artificial neural network has only one single layer. It is a category that is fully connected to the following layer where each node is attached to the others. It propagates the information in one direction from the inputs to the outputs through the hidden layer. This process is known as the front propagated wave that usually uses what is called the activation function. This activation function processes the data in each node of the layers. This neural network returns a sum of weights by the inputs calculated according to the hidden layer's activation function. The category of feedforward neural network usually uses the backpropagation method for the training process and the logistic function as an activation function.

Several other neural networks are a derivation of this type of networks. For example, *the radial-basis-function neural* networks.

This is a feedforward neural network that depends on the radial basis function instead of the logistic function. This type of neural networks have two layers, wherein the inner layer, the features, and radial basis function are combined. The radial function computes the distance of each point to the relative center. This neural network is useful for continuous values to evaluate the distance from the target value.

In contrast, the logistic function is used for mapping arbitrary binary values (i.e., 0 or 1; yes or no). *Deep feedforward neural networks* are a multilayer feedforward neural network. They became the most commonly used neural network types used in Machine Learning as they yield better results. A new type of learning called deep learning has emerged from this type of neural networks.

Recurrent neural networks are another category that uses a different type of nodes. Like a feedforward neural network, each hidden layer processes the information to the next layer. However, outputs of the hidden layers are saved and processed back to the previous layer. The first layer, comprised of the input layer, is processed as the product of the sum of the weighted features. The recurrent process is applied in hidden layers. At each step, every node will save information from the previous step. It uses memory, while the computation is running. In short, the recurrent neural network uses forward propagation and backpropagation to self-learn from the previous time steps to improve the predictions. In other words, information is processed in two directions, unlike the feedforward neural networks.

A multilayer perceptron, or multilayer neural network, is a neural network that has at least three or more layers. This category of networks is fully connected where every node is attached to all other nodes in the following layers.

Convolutional neural networks are typically useful for image classification or recognition. The processing used by this type of artificial neural network is designed to deal with pixel data. The convolutional neural networks are a multi-layer network that is based on convolutions, which apply filters for neuron activation. When the same filter is applied to a neuron, it leads to an activation of the same feature and results in what is called a feature map. The feature map reflects the strength and importance of a feature of input data.

Modular neural networks are formed from more than one connected neural network. These networks rely on the concept of 'divide and conquer.' They are handy for very complex problems because they allow combining different types of neural networks. Therefore, they allow combining the strengths of a different neural network to solve a complex problem where each neural network can handle a specific task.

How to train an artificial neural network?

As explained at the beginning of this chapter, neural networks compute a weighted sum of inputs and apply an activation function at each layer. Then it provides the final result to the output layer. This procedure is commonly named *forward propagation*. To train these artificial neural networks, weights need to be optimized to obtain the optimal weights that produce the most accurate outputs. The process of the training an artificial neural network is as follows:

1. Initialize the weights
2. Apply the forward propagation process
3. Evaluate the neural network performance
4. Apply the backward propagation process

5. Update the weights
6. Repeat the steps from step 2 until it attains a maximum number of iterations, or neural network performance does not improve.

As we can see from the steps of training an artificial neural network presented above, we need a performance measure that describes how accurate the neural network is. This function is called the loss function or cost function. This function can be the same as the cost function we presented in the previous chapter:

$$J = \frac{1}{N}\sum \left(y_{predicted} - y_{target}\right)^2$$

Where N is the number of outputs, $y_{predicted}$ is the output and y_{target} is the true value of the output. This function provides the error of the neural network. Small values of J reflect the high accuracy of the neural network.

So far, we defined loss function and how the neural network works in general. Now, let's go into the details for each step of the training process.

Let's consider a set of inputs X and outputs Y. We initialize W (i.e., weights) and B (i.e., bias) as a null matrix. The next step is to apply the feed-forward propagation that consists of feeding each layer of the artificial neural network with the sum of the weights by the inputs and the bias. Let's consider that we have two layers. We can calculate the first hidden layer's output using the following equation:

$$Z_1 = W_1 X + b_1$$

where W1 and b1 are the parameters of the neural network as the weights and bias of the first layer, respectively.

Next, we apply the activation function F1, that can be any activation from the function presented previously in this chapter:

$$A_1 = F_1(Z_1)$$

The result is the output of the first layer, which is then fed to the next layer as:

$$Z_2 = W_2 A_1 + b_2$$

with W2 and b2 are the weights and bias of the second layer, respectively.

To this result, we apply an activation function F2:

$$A_2 = F_2(Z_2)$$

Now A2 is supposed to be the output of the artificial neural network. The activation function F1 and F2 might be the same activation function or different activation function depending on the dataset and the expected output.

After the feedforward propagation, we compare the neural network output against the target output with the loss function. It is highly likely the difference between the estimated output and the actual values at this stage is very high. Therefore, we have to adjust the weights through the backpropagation process. We calculate the gradient of each activation function concerning biases and weights. We start by evaluating the derivative of the last layer, then the layer before this layer on so on until the input layer. Then update the weights according to the gradient or the derivative of the activation function. Applying these steps to our example of two layers neural network it provides:

$$W_2 = W_2 - \alpha \frac{d}{dW} F_2(W, b)$$

$$b_2 = b_2 - \alpha \frac{d}{db} F_2(W, b)$$

$$W_1 = W_1 - \alpha \frac{d}{dW} F_2(W, b)$$

$$b_1 = b_1 - \alpha \frac{d}{db} F_2(W, b)$$

The parameter α is the learning rate parameter. This parameter determines the rate by which the weights are updated. The process that we just describe here is called the gradient descent algorithm. The process is repeated until it attains a pre-fixed maximum number of iterations. In chapter 4, we will develop an example to illustrate a perceptron and multi-layer neural network by following similar steps using Python. We will develop a classifier based on an artificial neural network. Now, let's explore the pros of using an artificial neural network for Machine Learning applications.

Artificial neural network: pros and cons of use

Nowadays, artificial neural networks are applied in almost every domain. Research in the domain of artificial neural networks is very active, and several neural networks immerged to take advantage of the full potential of this Artificial intelligence approach. Artificial neural networks have several advantages.

Artificial neural networks are able to map structures and learn from the data faster. They are also able to map the complex structure and connections that relate the outputs to the input datasets, which is the case in many real-life applications. Once an artificial neural network is developed and trained, it can be generalized. In other words, it can be applied to map relationships between data that it has not been exposed to or to make predictions for new datasets. Moreover, the artificial neural network does not make any assumptions of the structure or the distribution of the input data. It does not impose specific conditions on the data or assumptions on the relationship in the data, unlike traditional statistical methods. The fact that artificial neural networks can handle a large amount of data makes them an appealing tool. Artificial neural networks are a non-parametric approach that allows developing a model with a reduced error that is caused by the estimation of the parameters. Although these appealing characteristics of artificial neural networks, they suffer from some drawbacks.

The downside of artificial neural networks is that they often operate as a black box. This means that we cannot fully understand the relationship between the inputs and outputs and the interdependence between specific input variables and the output. In other words, we cannot detect how much each input variable impacts the output. The training process can be computationally inefficient. We can overcome this problem by using parallel computing and taking advantage of the computation power of computers by using proper coding.

Conclusion

Thanks for reading to the end!

Python Machine Learning may be the answer that you are looking for when it comes to all of these needs and more. It is a simple process that can teach your machine how to learn on its own, similar to what the human mind can do, but much faster and more efficient. It has been a game-changer in many industries, and this guidebook tried to show you the exact steps that you can take to make this happen.

There is just so much that a programmer can do when it comes to using Machine Learning in their coding, and when you add it together with the Python coding language, you can take it even further, even as a beginner.

The next step is to start putting some of the knowledge that we discussed in this guidebook to good use. There are a lot of great things that you can do when it comes to Machine Learning, and when we can combine it with the Python language, there is nothing that we can't do when it comes to training our machine or our computer.

This guidebook took some time to explore a lot of the different things that you can do when it comes to Python Machine Learning. We looked at what Machine Learning is all about, how to work with it, and even a crash course on using the Python language for the first time. Once that was done, we moved right into combining the two of these to work with a variety of Python libraries to get the work done.

If you have ever wanted to learn how to work with the Python coding language, or you want to see what Machine Learning can do for you, then this guidebook is the ultimate tool that you need! Take a chance to read through it and see just how powerful Python Machine Learning can be for you.

Python Data Science

The Ultimate and Complete Beginners Guide to Master Data Science with Python Step by Step

Table of Contents

INTRODUCTION **141**

HISTORY OF DATA SCIENCE **149**

WORKING WITH PYTHON FOR DATA SCIENCE **153**

WHAT IS PYTHON? 154
PYTHON'S POSITION IN DATA SCIENCE..155
PYTHON INSTALLATION 157
INSTALLATION UNDER WINDOWS.. 158
INSTALLATION UNDER MAC..159
INSTALLATION UNDER LINUX 159
PYTHON ENGINEERING STRUCTURE 162

MACHINE LEARNING AND HOW IT FITS WITH DATA SCIENCE **165**

WHAT IS MACHINE LEARNING? 166

DATA STRUCTURES & OBJECT-ORIENTED PYTHON **171**

IMMUTABLE STRUCTURED DATA (STATIC)...172
INDEXING, TRIMMING AND OTHER TUPLE OPERATIONS 182
TUPLE METHODS..187
ZIP FUNCTION 188
FROZEN SETS (FROZEN SET).. 188
INDEXING, TRIMMING AND OTHER LIST OPERATIONS 191
OBJECT-ORIENTED PROGRAMMING WITH PYTHON.............................195

DATA SCIENCE ALGORITHMS AND MODELS **201**

NEURAL NETWORKS 201
NAÏVE BAYES 204
CLUSTERING ALGORITHMS 205
SUPPORT VECTOR MACHINES 206
DECISION TREES..208
K-NEAREST NEIGHBORS...209
THE MARKOV ALGORITHM 210

REGRESSION ANALYSIS (LINEAR REGRESSION AND LOGISTIC REGRESSION) 213
- LINEAR REGRESSION 214
- LOGISTIC REGRESSION 218
- LOGISTIC REGRESSION VS. LINEAR REGRESSION 222
- HOW DOES MACHINE LEARNING COMPARE TO AI 223

DATA AGGREGATION AND GROUP OPERATIONS 227
- WHAT IS DATA AGGREGATION 228

PRACTICAL CODES AND EXERCISES TO USE PYTHON 231

FUNCTIONS AND MODULES IN PYTHON 241
- THE SYNTAX OF FUNCTIONS 241
- HOW FUNCTIONS ARE CALLED IN PYTHON 242

INTERACTION WITH DATABASES 245

DATA MINING TECHNIQUES IN DATA SCIENCE 253
- MAPREDUCE TECHNIQUE 253
- DISTANCE MEASURES 254
- LINK ANALYSIS 254
- PAGERANK 255
- THE CONTENT 255
- DATA STREAMING 255
- SAMPLING DATA IN A STREAM 256
- FILTERING STREAMS 256
- COUNT SPECIFIC ELEMENTS IN A STREAM 257
- FREQUENT ITEM – SET ANALYSIS 257

DATA IN THE CLOUD 259
- WHAT IS THE CLOUD? 259
- NETWORK 259
- DATA SCIENCE IN THE CLOUD 260
- SOFTWARE ARCHITECTURE AND QUALITY ATTRIBUTES 262
- SHARING BIG DATA IN THE CLOUD 262

CONCLUSION 265

Introduction

When it comes to the locations and sources where a business can collect data there are quite a few options that are open to the business. Many businesses will hire data scientists to help them collect this information from sources like social media, sensors, digital videos, and pictures, purchased transactions that they get from their customers and even from surveys that the customers may have taken.

Because there are so many sources that the company can focus on when it comes to getting the information they want, it won't take much research before the company becomes flooded with all of the presented data. There is just so much data available, which is great, but we have to make sure that we know the right steps to handle the info and to learn what is there, rather than just collecting the information and calling it good.

The analysis that you will do on all of that data that comes in is a big part of data science. All this helps us to bring together a lot of professional skills to handle that info and put it to good use. Yes, it is going to include searching for the info so it is a good idea to not forget it or skip over this part, but it can come in and help with understanding the info as well. To get all of this done, we need to have a few skills come together, either in one person or within the team, to make data science useful. Some of the things that data science, and the info we collect, will be able to help us out with will include.

- Reducing the number of costs that the business has to deal with.
- Helping to launch a brand new service or product and knowing it will do well.

- To help gauge the effectiveness that we see in a new marketing campaign.
- To help tap into some different demographics along the way.
- To ensure that we can get into a new market and see success.

Of course, this is not an extensive list that we can look at, and knowing the right steps and all of the benefits that come with working in data science can help us to see some improvements and can make the business grow. No matter what items or services you sell, what your geographic location is, or what industry you are in you can use data science to help your business become more successful.

Sometimes, it is hard for companies to see how they can use data science to help improve themselves. We may assume that this is just a bunch of hype, or that only a few companies have been able to see success with it. However, there are a ton of companies that can use this kind of information to get themselves ahead, including some of the big names like Amazon, Visa, and Google. While your business may or may not be on the same level as those three, it is still possible for you to put data science to work for your needs, improving what you can offer on the market, how you can help customers out, and so much more.

It is important to note that data science is a field that is already taking over the world, and it is helping companies in many different areas. For example, it is showing companies the best way to grow, how to reach their customers correctly and most efficiently, how to find new sources of value, and so much more. It often depends on the overall goal of the company for using this process of data science to determine what they will get out of it.

With all of the benefits that come with using this process of data science, and all of the big-name companies who are jumping on board and trying to gain some of the knowledge and benefits as well, we need to take a look at the life cycle that comes with data science, and the steps that it takes to make this project a big success. Let's dive into some of the things that we need to know about the data life cycle so we know the basics of what needs to happen to see success with data science.

Data discovery

The first step that we are going to see with this life cycle is the idea that companies need to get out there and discover the info they want to use. This is the phase where we will search in a lot of different sources in order to discover the data that we need. Sometimes the data are going to be structured, such as in text format but other times it may come in a more unstructured format like videos and images. There are even some times when the data we find comes to us as a relational database system instead.

These are going to be considered some of the more traditional ways that you can collect the info that you need, but it is also possible for an organization to explore some different options as well. For example, many companies are relying on social media to help them reach their customers and to gain a better understanding of the mindset and buying decisions of these customers through this option.

Often this phase is going to include us starting with a big question that we would like answered, and then searching either for the data in the first place or if we already have the data, searching through the info that we have already collected. This makes it easier for us to get through all of that data and gain the insights that we are looking for.

Getting the data prepared

After we spend some time going through all of the different sources to find the information that we need, it is time to look at how we can use these data, and data preparation will help out with this. There are a few steps that happen in this phase, basically we are going to do things like converting the information from all of those different sources into one common format so that they work together, and an algorithm that we pick out later will be able to handle the data without errors or mistakes.

This process is going to be more involved, but it is where the data scientist will start collecting clean subsets of data and then will insert the defaults and the parameters that are needed for you. In some cases, the methods that you use will be more complex, like identifying some of the values that are missing out of that data, and more.

Another step that needs to happen while you are here is to clean off the data. This is so important when you collect the data from more than one source because it ensures that it's the same and that the algorithm you pick will be able to read it all later. You also want to make sure that there isn't any information missing, that the duplicate values are gone, and there is nothing else found within the set of data you want to work with that will decrease the accuracy of the model that you are trying to make.

After you go through and clean off the data you would like to use, the next step is to do the integration and then create our conclusion based on the set of data for the analysis. This analysis is going to involve taking the data and then merging two or more tables that have the same objects, but different information. It can also include the process of aggregation, which is when we summarize the different fields found in the table as we go through the process.

During this whole process, the goal is for us to explore and then come up with an understanding of the patterns, as well as the values, that are going to show up in the data set that we are working with. This can take some time and some patience, but it is going to ensure that any mathematical models we work with later make sense and work the way that we want.

Mathematical models

When working with data science, all of the projects that you will want to work with will need to use mathematical models to help them get it all done. These are models that we can plan out ahead of time and then the data scientist is going to build them up to help suit the needs of the business or the question that they would like answered. In some cases, it is possible to work with a few different areas that fall in the world of mathematics, including linear regression, statistics, and logistics, to get these models done.

To get all of this done, we also have to make sure we are using the right tools and methods to make it easier. Some of the computing tools for statistics that come with R can help as well as working with some other advanced analytical tools, SQL, and Python, and any visualization tool that you need to make sure the data makes sense.

Also, we have to make sure that we are getting results that are satisfactory out of all the work and sometimes that means we need to bring in more than one algorithm or model to see the results. In this case, the data scientist has to go through and create a group of models that can work together to go through that info and answer any of the questions that the business has.

After measuring out the models that they would like to use, the data scientist can then revise some of the parameters that are in place, and do the fine-tuning that is needed as they go through the next round of modeling. This process is going to take up a few rounds to complete because you have to test it out more than once to make sure that it's going to work the way that you would like it to.

Putting it all into action

At this point, we have had a chance to prepare the data the way that it needs to be done, and we have been able to build up some of the models that we want to us. With this in mind, it is time to work with the models to get them to provide us with the kinds of results that need to show up. It is possible, depending on the data you have the model you choose to go with, that there will be a few discrepancies, and you may have to go through a few levels of troubleshooting to deal with the process, but this is normal. Most data scientists have to make some changes to their models as they go through the process before coming up with the solution that is right for them.

Of course, to see how the model is going to play out in the real world, we need to first test out the model. This is the best way to see what will happen when the model is in use, rather than just a theory. You can try out a new algorithm with it as well to see if one type is a better option than any of the others. Sometimes, this is the part where we will decide to put in more than one algorithm to handle our data needs.

The importance of communication

While we are going through this life cycle of data, we need to spend a few moments talking about how important communication can be to the whole process. A good data scientist, or a good team of data scientists, is not going to be just working with the algorithms and the numbers; they are also going to handle the communication that has to go on. There is someone on the business end, such as the marketers and key decision-makers who will need to be able to read through this information, and the data scientist needs to be able to communicate in a manner that is easy to understand.

Communicating what has been found inside of the data, and through the various algorithms used, is going to be one of the important steps that we need to use in the data life cycle. During this stage, the professional is going to be able to talk between the different teams that are present, and they have to be skilled enough to communicate and to share their findings clearly and concisely.

Many different people need to have this kind of information, and not all of them are going to be data scientists or people who can understand some of the technical parts that come into play. The data scientist still has to share this information to make sure that these key decision-makers can understand the information and what insights have been found in the data. The decision-makers can then take that information and use it to decide which direction to take their company.

One thing to keep in mind here though is that a data scientist has to make sure that they are doing this communication in many different ways. Often this can include the written and the spoken word, so get ready to work on some of those public speaking skills and interpersonal skills to get things done.

But the written and the spoken words are not going to be the only places where the data scientist is going to need to know how to communicate. For example, the last part that comes with data science and its lifecycle is some kind of visualization of the information and the insights that are found in all that data. These visualizations can take all of the numbers and all of the data, and put it into some kind of image, like a bar chart, a graph, a pie chart or some other method or image.

This is useful because it can take a lot of information and put it into a form that we can just glance at and understand. Instead of having to go through all of the different pieces of information, and reading through all of that data, we can use these images to make it easier to see and understand what is going on, what relationships showed up for each part, and so much more.

The data life cycle is so important to help you understand what is in all of that data that you have collected over time. Companies can collect more data than ever, but they need to know how to take it and turn it into a form that can be used. This is often easier said than done, but by working with the life cycle of data that we talked about previously, you will be able to not only collect all of the data but also put it to good use to make some good business decisions.

History of Data Science

The history of deep learning can be traced back to 1943, when Warren McCulloch and Walter Pitts published a paper with a concept of Artificial Neuron (AN) to mimic the thought process. This Artificial Neuron was based on the characteristic of a biological neuron of either being fully active to stimulation or none at all. This behavior of biological neuron was observed in microelectrode readings from the brain.

In 1957, Frank and Rosenblatt presented Mark I Perceptron Machine as the first implementation of the perceptron algorithm. The idea was to resemble the working of a biological neuron to create an agent that can learn. This perceptron was a supervised binary linear classifier with adjustable weights. This functionality was implemented through the following function:

$$f(x) = \begin{cases} 1, & wX + B > 0 \\ 0, & otherwise \end{cases}$$

Where w is the weights vector, X is the input and b is the bias.

For each input and output pair, this formula provided classification results given by $f(x)$, the predicted value/output of the function.

In 1960, Widrow and Hoff stacked these perceptrons and built a 3-layered (input layer, hidden layer, output layer), fully connected, feed-forward architecture for classification as a hardware implementation, called ADALINE.

In 1960, Henry J. Kelley introduced a continuous back propagation model, which is currently used in the learning weights of the model. In 1962, a simpler version of backpropagation based on chain rule was introduced by Stuart Dreyfus but these methods were inefficient. The backpropagation currently used in models was presented in the 1980s.

In 1979, Fukushima designed a multi-layered Convolutional Neural Network architecture, called Neocognitron, that could learn to recognize patterns in images. The network was similar to current day architectures but wasn't exactly the same. It also allowed to manually adjust the weight of certain connections. Many concepts from Neocognitron continue to be used. The layered connections in perceptrons sere useful to develop a variety of neural networks. For several patterns present in the data, the Selective Attention Model could distinguish and separate them.

In 1970, Seppo Linnainmaa presented automatic differentiation to efficiently compute the derivative of a differentiable composite function using the chain rule. Its application, later in 1986, led to the backpropagation of errors in multilayer perceptrons. This was when Geoff Hinton, Williams and Rumelhart presented a paper to demonstrate that backpropagation in neural networks provides interesting distribution representations. In 1989, Yann LeCun, currently, Director of AI Research Facebook, provided the first practical demonstration of backpropagation in Convolutional Neural Networks to read handwritten digits at Bell Labs.

Even though with backpropagation, deep neural networks were not being able to train well.

In 1995, Vapnik and Cortes introduced support vector machines for regression and classification of data. In 1997, Schmidhuber and Hochreiter introduced Long Short Term Memory (LSTM) for recurrent neural networks.

In all these years, a major hindering constraint was computed but in

1999, computers started to become faster at processing data and Graphical Processing Units (GPUs) were introduced. This immensely increased the compute power.

In 2006, Hinton and Salakhutdinov presented a paper that reinvigorated research in deep learning. This was the first time when a proper 10 layer Convolutional Neural Network was trained properly. Instead of training 10 layers using backpropagation, they came up with an unsupervised pre-training scheme, called Restricted Boltzmann Machine. This was a 2 step approach for training. In the first step, each layer of the network was trained using unsupervised objective. In the second step, all the layers were stacked together for backpropagation.

Later in 2009, Fei-Fei Li, a professor at Stanford University launched ImageNet, a large visual database designed for visual object recognition research containing more than 14 million hand-annotated images of 20,000 different object categories. This gave neural networks a huge edge as data of this order made it possible to train neural networks and achieve good results.

In 2010, neural networks got a lot of attention from the research community when Microsoft presented a paper on speech recognition and neural networks performed really well compared to other Machine Learning tools like SVMs and kernels. Specifically, they introduced neural networks as a part of the GMM and HMM framework and achieved huge improvements.

In 2012, a paper by Krizhevsky, Sutskever and Hinton showed that huge improvements are achieved through deep learning in the visual recognition domain. Their model, AlexNet outperformed all the other traditional computer vision methods in visual recognition tasks and won several international competitions. Since then, the field has exploded and several network architectures and ideas have been introduced like GANs.

Working with Python for Data Science

Programming languages help us to expand our theoretical knowledge to something that can happen. Data science, which usually needs a lot of data to make things happen, will by nature take advantage of programming languages to make the data organize well for further steps of the model development. So, let us start learning about Python for a better understanding of the topic.

Why Python Is Important?

To illustrate this problem more vividly, we might as well assume that we have a small partner named Estella. She just got a job related to Data Science after graduating from the math department. On her first day at work, she was enthusiastic and eager to get in touch with this dude-new industry. But she soon found herself facing a huge difficulty:

The data needed to process the work is not stored in her personal computer, but in remote servers, some in traditional relational databases, and some in Hadoop clusters. Unlike Windows, which is mostly used by personal computers, Linux-like systems are used on remote servers. Estella is not used to this operating system because the familiar graphical interface is missing. All operations, such as the simplest reading of files, need to be programmed by oneself. Therefore, Estella is eager to find a programming language that is simple to write, easy to learn and easy to use.

What is more fatal is that the familiar data modeling software, such as SPSS and MATLAB, cannot be used in the new working environment. However, Estella often uses some basic algorithms provided by this software in her daily work, such as linear regression and logical regression. Therefore, she hopes that the programming language she finds will also have a library of algorithms that can be used easily, and of course, it is better to be free of charge.

The whole process is very similar to Estella's favorite table tennis. The assumption is sent to the data as a "ball", and then the adjustment is made according to the "return ball" of the data, and the above actions are repeated. Therefore, Estella added one more item to her request: the programming language can be modified and used at any time without compilation. It is better to have an immediate response command window so that she can quickly verify her ideas. After a search, Estella excitedly told everyone that she had found an IT tool that met all her requirements that is Python.

I hope you have got a good layman introduction on why programming language is important for Data Science. In the next sections, we will describe the language and its basic functions in detail.

What Is Python?

Python is an object-oriented and interpretive computer program language. Its syntax is simple and contains a set of standard libraries with complete functions, which can easily accomplish many common tasks. Speaking of Python, its birth is also quite interesting. During the Christmas holidays in 1989, Dutch programmer Guido van Rossum stayed at home and found himself doing nothing. So, to pass the "boring" time, he wrote the first version of Python.

Python is widely used. According to statistics from GitHub, an open-source community, it has been one of the most popular programming languages in the past 10 years and is more popular than traditional C, C++ languages and C# which is very commonly used in Windows systems. After using Python for some time, Estella thinks it is a programming language specially designed for non-professional programmers.

Its grammatical structure is very concise, encouraging everyone to write as much code as possible that is easy to understand and write as little code as possible.

Functionally speaking, Python has a large number of standard libraries and third-party libraries. Estella develops her application based on these existing programs, which can get twice the result with half the effort and speed up the development progress.

More conveniently, Python can be shipped across platforms. For example, Estella often writes Python code under his familiar Windows system and then deploys the developed program to the server of the Linux system. To sum up, in one sentence Python is studious and easy to use.

Python's Position in Data Science

After mastering Python as a programming language, Estella can do many interesting things, such as writing a web crawler, collecting needed data from the Internet, developing a task scheduling system, updating the model regularly, etc.

Below we will describe how Python is used by Estella for Data Science applications:

Data Cleaning

After obtaining the original data, Estella will first do preliminary processing on the data, such as unifying the case of the string, correcting the wrong data, etc. This is also the so-called "clean up" of "dirty" data to make the data more suitable for analysis. With Python and its third-party library pandas, Estella can easily complete this step of work.

Data Visualization

Estella uses Matplotlib to display data graphically. Before extracting the features, Estella can get the first intuitive feeling of the data from the graph and enlighten the thinking. When communicating with colleagues in other departments, information can be clearly and effectively conveyed and communicated with the help of graphics, so those insights can be put on paper.

Feature Extraction

In this step, Richard usually associates relevant data stored in different places, for example, integrating customer basic information and customer shopping information through customer ID. Then transform the data and extract the variables useful for modeling. These variables are called features. In this process, Estella will use Python's NumPy, SciPy, pandas, and PySpark.

Model Building

The open-source libraries sci-kit-learn, StatsModels, Spark ML, and TensorFlow cover almost all the commonly used basic algorithms. Based on these algorithm bases and according to the data characteristics and algorithm assumptions, Estella can easily build the basic algorithms together and create the model she wants.

The above four things are also the four core steps in Data Science. No wonder Estella, like most other data scientists, chose Python as a tool to complete his work.

Python Installation

After introducing so many advantages of Python, let's quickly install it and feel it for ourselves.

Python has two major versions: Python 2 and Python 3. Python 3 is a higher version with new features that Python 2 does not have. However, because Python 3 was not designed with backward compatibility in mind, Python 2 was still the main product in actual production (although Python 3 had been released for almost 10 years at the time of writing this book). Therefore, it is recommended that readers still use Python 2 when installing completely. The code accompanying this book is compatible with Python 2 and Python 3.

The following describes how to install Python and the libraries listed in section

It should be noted that the distributed Machine Learning library Spark ML involves the installation of Java and Scala, and will not be introduced here for the time being.

Installation Under Windows

The author does not recommend people to develop under Windows system. There are many reasons, the most important of which is that in the era of big data, as mentioned by Estella earlier, data are stored under the Linux system. Therefore, in production, the programs developed by data scientists will eventually run in the Linux environment. However, the compatibility between Windows and Linux is not good, which easily leads to the development and debugging of good programs under Windows, and cannot operate normally under the actual production environment.

If the computer the reader uses is a Windows system, he can choose to install a Linux virtual machine and then develop it on the virtual machine. If readers insist on using Windows, due to the limitation of TensorFlow under Windows, they can only choose to install Python 3.5 (as of the time of writing this book). Therefore, the tutorial below this section is also different from other sections, using Python 3. Anaconda installed several applications under Windows, such as IPython, Jupyter, Conda, and Spyder. Below we will explain some of them in detail.

Conda

It is a management system for the Python development environment and open source libraries. If readers are familiar with Linux, Conda is equivalent to pip+virtualenv under Linux. Readers can list installed Python libraries by entering "Condolist" on the command line.

Spyder

It is an integrated development environment (IDE) specially designed for Python for scientific computing. If readers are familiar with the mathematical analysis software MATLAB, they can find that Spyder and MATLAB are very similar in syntax and interface.

Installation Under MAC

Like Anaconda's version of Windows, Anaconda's Mac version does not contain a deep learning library TensorFlow, which needs to be installed using pip(Python Package Management System). Although using pip requires a command line, it is very simple to operate and even easier than installing Anaconda. Moreover, pip is more widely used, so it is suggested that readers try to install the required libraries with pip from the beginning. The installation method without Anaconda is described below.

Starting with Mac OS X 10.2, Python is preinstalled on macs. For learning purposes, you can choose to use the pre-installed version of Python ; directly. If it is for development purposes, pre-installed Python is easy to encounter problems when installing third-party libraries, and the latest version of Python needs to be reinstalled. The reader is recommended to reinstall Python here.

Installation Under Linux

Similar to Mac, Anaconda also offers Linux versions. Please refer to the instructions under Windows and the accompanying code for specific installation steps.

There are many versions of Linux, but due to space limitations, the only installation on Ubuntu is described here. The following installation guide may also run on other versions of Linux, but we have only tested these installation steps on Ubuntu 14.04 or later.

Although Ubuntu has pre-installed Python, the version is older, and it is recommended to install a newer version of Python.

Install Python

```
install [insert command here]
```

Pip is a Python software package management system that facilitates us to install the required third-party libraries. The steps for installing pip are as follows.

1) Open the terminal

2) Enter and run the following code

```
python shell
```

Python, as a dynamic language, is usually used in two ways: it can be used as a script interpreter to run edited program scripts; At the same time, Python provides a real-time interactive command window (Python shell) in which any Python statement can be entered and run. This makes it easy to learn, debug, and test Python statements.

Enter "python" in the terminal (Linux or Mac) or command prompt (Windows) to start the Python shell.

You can assign values to variables in the Python shell and then calculate the variables used. And you can always use these variables as long as you don't close the shell. As shown in lines 1 to 3 of the code. It is worth noting that Python is a so-called dynamic type language, so there is no need to declare the type of a variable when assigning values to variables.

Any Python statement can be run in the Python shell, as shown in the code, so some people even use it as a calculator.

You can also import and use a third-party library in the shell, as shown. It should be noted that as shown in the code, the third-party library "numpy" can be given an alias, such as "np" while being imported. When "numpy" is needed later, it is replaced by "np" to reduce the amount of character input.

1) Here are 3 special practical tips.

   1. Use the type function to get the type of the calling object. The dir function is used to obtain all the attributes and methods of the calling object, as shown in lines 10 and 12 of the code.

   2. Every object (class, function) in Python has a default "__doc__" variable (it is worth noting that "doc" is double underlined before and after), which records the instruction of the object, as shown in line 14 of the code.

   3. When we are not familiar with the objects used, these three methods can help us to understand them quickly.

Programming code is here for the concept we are discussing:

```
directory [ import command here]
{insert variables here}
[command to print]
[enter function here]
[help function]
```

In the previous installation steps, we installed the interactive interpreter IPython. It is similar to the Python shell described above, but it provides more powerful editing and interactive functions, such as the automatic Tab key. Similarly, input "iPython" at the terminal to start it and recommend it to readers.

Python Engineering Structure

This section discusses the engineering structure of Python projects. This part of the content for beginners may be more abstract. If readers find the following text difficult to understand, they can skip this section first, which does not affect the reading of other chapters in this book.

Suppose Estella has developed some scripts and put them in a file directory. Now, as a reader, when developing a new project, you hope to reuse the previous code like using a third-party library like NumPy. How should this be achieved? The answer is to create an __init__.py file full of "magic." Specifically, look at the following example.

First, create a mini_project directory with two subdirectories: components and tests. However, there are two Python scripts under components, namely counter.py and selecter.py.

1) wordCount function is defined in counter.py script.

2) getFrequentItem function is defined in selecter.py

This function depends on the wordCount function mentioned above, so import it at the beginning of the script with the following command:

| [command for input] counter [to get] function |

3) tests/test _ selector.py is the entrance to the program, that is, the script to be run directly, which will call the getFrequentItem function. Similarly, import getFrequentItem at the beginning of this script.

| [command for input] frequency [to get] function |

If you use the "Python test _ selector.py" command to run the program at this time, you will get the following error prompt:

| error: not present as a module |

This is because Python does not regard the directory mini_project as a usable library, so the import failed. To fix this bug, just create an empty __init__.py file in each directory.

In essence, Python's library is a directory containing __init__.py files. __init__.py defines the properties and methods of this library. When we use the import command to import a library, we are importing the init__.py file. Under normal circumstances, there is no need to define anything in it, only an empty file is needed, Python will automatically process according to the default settings.

But without this file, Python would not regard the corresponding directory as a third-party library, and we would not be able to import and use it.

It is also worth reminding that when importing a library, you need to ensure that its corresponding directory is visible under the system path. To put it more bluntly, the corresponding library directory can be found under "sys.path." If not, then the corresponding path needs to be added to "sys. path"

By this we have given a complete introduction to Python and why it can be considered as a good option for Data Science. In the next chapter, we will look at Python operations more in detail. This learning can help us with great Data Science projects. So why are you waiting? Let us get a dive into it.

Machine Learning and How It Fits with Data Science

The next topic that we need to take a look at is Machine Learning and how it comes into play when we work with Data Science and all of the neat things that we can do with this topic. Machine learning can definitely be an important part of the Data Science process, as long as we use it properly.

Remember as we go through this process that part of Data Science is working on data analysis. This helps us to take a lot of the data we have collected along the way, and then actually see the insights and the predictions that are inside of it. To make this happen, we need to be able to create our models (that can sort through all of the data), find the hidden patterns, and provide us with our insights.

To define these models, and to make sure that they work the way that we want, we need to have a variety of good algorithms in place, and this is where Machine Learning is going to come into play quite a bit. You will find that with the help of Machine Learning, and the variety of algorithms that are present in Machine Learning, we can create models that can go through any kind of data we have, whether it is big or small, and provide us with the answers that we need here.

Machine learning is a process that we can use to make the system or the machine we are working with think in a manner that humans do. This allows the algorithm to go through and find hidden patterns in the same manner that a human would be able to do, but it can do it much faster and more efficiently than any human could do manually.

Think about how hard this would be to do manually for any human, or even for a group of people who are trying to get through all of that data. It could take them years to get through all of that data and find the insights that they need. And with how fast data are being generated and collected, those predictions and insights would be worthless by the time we got to that point anyway.

Machine learning can make this process so much easier. It allows us to have a way to think through the data and find the hidden patterns and insights that are inside for our needs. With the right Machine Learning algorithm, we can learn how the process works, and all of the steps that are necessary to make this happen for us. With this in mind, it is time to take a closer look at Machine Learning, and all of the parts that we need to know to make this work for our needs.

What is Machine Learning?

The first thing that we need to take a look at here is the basics of Machine Learning. Machine learning is going to be one of the applications of artificial intelligence that can provide a system with the ability to learn, all on its own, without the help of a programmer telling the system what to do. The system can even take this a bit further and can work to improve based on its own experience, and none of this is done with the system being explicitly programmed in the process. The idea of Machine Learning is going to be done with a focus on the development of programs on the computer that can access any data you have, and can then use that presented data to learn something new, and how you would like it to behave.

There are going to be a few different applications that we can look at when it comes to using Machine Learning. As we start to explore more about what Machine Learning can do, you may notice that over the years, it has been able to change and develop into something that programmers are going to enjoy working with more than ever. When you want to make your machine or system do a lot of the work on its own, without you having to step in and program every step, then Machine Learning is the right option for you.

When it comes to the world of technology, we will find that Machine Learning is pretty unique and can add to a level of fun to the coding that we do. There are already a lot of companies, in a variety of industries (which we will talk about in a bit), that will use Machine Learning and are already receiving a ton of benefits from it.

There are a lot of different applications when it comes to using Machine Learning, and it is amazing what all we can do with this kind of artificial intelligence. Some of the best methods that we can follow and focus our time on when it comes to Machine Learning include:

1. *Research on statistics:* Machine learning is already making some headway when it comes to the world of IT. You will find that Machine Learning can help you go through a ton of complex data, looking for the large and important patterns that are in the data. Some of the different applications of Machine Learning under this category will include things like spam filtering, credit cards, and search engines.

2. *An analysis of big data:* There are a lot of companies who have spent time collecting what is known as Big Data, and now they have to find a way to sort through and learn from that data, in a short amount of time. Companies can use these data to learn more about how money is spent by the customers, and even to help them make important decisions about the future. If we had someone go through and manually do the work, it would take much too long. But with Machine Learning, we can get it all done. Options like the medical field, election

campaigns, and even retail stores have started to turn to Machine Learning to gain some of these benefits.

3. *The financial world:* Many financial companies have been able to rely on Machine Learning. Stock trading online, for example, will rely on this kind of work, and we will find that Machine Learning can help with fraud detection, loan approvals, and more.

To help us get going with this one, and to understand how we can receive the value that we want out of Machine Learning, we have to make sure that we pair the best algorithms with the right processes and tools. If you are using the wrong kind of algorithm to sort through these data, you are going to get a lot of inaccurate information, and the results will not give you the help that you need. Working with the right algorithm the whole time will make a big difference.

The cool thing that we will see with this one is that there are a lot of Machine Learning algorithms that we can choose from at this point to work on your model. Each of these works in a different manner than the others, but this ensures that you can handle any kind of problem that comes along with your project. With this in mind though, you will notice that some of the different available algorithms include random forests, neural networks, clustering, support vector machines, and more.

As we are working on some of the models that we want to produce, we will also notice that there are a ton of tools and other processes that are available for us to work with. We need to make sure that we pick the right one to ensure that the algorithm and the model that you are working with will perform the way that you would like. The different tools that are available with Machine Learning will include:

1. Comprehensive management and data quality.

2. Automated ensemble evaluation of the model to help see where the best performers will show up.

3. GUIs for helping to build up the models that you want along with the process flows being built up as well.

4. Easy deployment of this so that you can get results that are reliable and repeatable in a quick manner.

5. Interactive exploration of the data and even some visualizations that help us to view the information easier.

6. A platform that is integrated and end to end to help with the automation of some of the data to decision process that you would like to follow.

7. A tool to compare the different models of Machine Learning to help us identify the best one to use quickly and efficiently.

Data Structures & Object-Oriented Python

For most of the examples, we have used simple data, which has a single value associated with it: an integer, a real or a Boolean. They are scalar objects because they are indivisible, that is, they do not have an accessible internal structure. We have also introduced composite data such as text or string of characters, represented by strings, as well as sequences in the form of lists that we use to cycle through elements in iterative compositions for. These types of data are not scalar because they can be divided into elements and accessed, they are structured data.

Structured or composite data contains elements, which can be simple data or other composite data. We remember that both simple and compound data in Python are treated as an object.

The elements can all be of the same type, such as strings containing characters, and in this case, they are called homogeneous structured data. Other languages (C/C ++, Matlab, Pascal) have homogeneous structures such as the array (array or table), very useful for operations with vectors or matrices. The standard Python does not have a structure such as an array of C or Pascal although the numerical Python library (NumPy) 20 does include these options.

In Python, the composite or structured data can be classified into two groups, according to the characteristic of whether or not their elements can be changed, reduced or expanded: *structured data mutable and immutable.*

Immutable structured data (static)

Immutable structured data, also called static or fixed values/size, are characterized in that the elements of their sequence cannot be changed or deleted. Nor can new elements be added to the data structure. If you want to modify this type of data, use the resource to create new value. In Python, we have as immutable structured data the character strings (string) and the tuples (tuple), as data streams, and the frozen sets (frozen set).

Character string – Indexing or access and sequence length

The elements (characters) of the string (or of any sequence) can be accessed through an index that is placed in square brackets, [index] and tells what position the element is inside the string.

For example,

```
>>> s = 'wooden house'
>>> letter_1 = s [0]
>>> long = len (s)
>>> last_letter = s [long-1] # alternative: s [-1]
>>> print (letter_1, last_ letter, long)
w e 12
```

The value 'wooden house' is a string type object, which includes a sequence of 12 characters. This value is assigned to the variable s, which refers to the same object. We access the first element with the index 0 (letter_1 = s [0]). As we indicated in the introduction of the lists, remember that in Python the first element of the sequences is at position 0 when indexed (accessed). To calculate the number of elements, or length, of the sequence of structured data we use the internal function len (). The chain has 12 elements and its last element is in position 11 (length - 1) or -1.

w	o	o	d	e	n		h	o	u	s	e
1	2	3	4	5	6	7	8	9	10	11	12
-12	-11	-10	-9	-8	-7	-6	-5	-4	-3	-2	-1

String elements and indexes to access them (positive and negative)

An empty string can be created: s = '' (two single quotes without space), len(s) = 0.

Trimming or slicing sequences and other operations

To extract a subset of elements (or segment) of a string or any sequence, the cutting operator [n: m] is used, where n is the first element to be extracted and m-1 the last.

Several examples of access to the elements and trimming segments of the string in the previous figure are presented. The comment indicates the result:

```
>>> s = 'wooden house'
>>> segm1 = s [0: 3] # segm1 <- 'woo'
>>> segm1 = s [: 3] # segm1 <- 'woo', equivalent to the previous slice
>>> segm2 = s [8: len (s)]  # segm2 <- 'hous'
>>> segm2 = s [8:] # segm2 <- 'hous', equivalent to the previous slice
>>> segm3 = s [0: 14: 2] # segm3 <- 'wo nhue', slice 0:12 in 2-in-2 steps
```

```
>>> letter_u = s [-1] # letter_u <- 'e', equals access
last element
>>> letter_penu = s [-2] # letter_penu <- 's',
equivalent to penultimate access elem
```

In the cutting operator, if the first index [: m] (before the colon) is omitted, trimming starts from the first element. If the second index [n:] is omitted, it is trimmed to the end of the sequence. Negative indexes are useful for accessing the last element [-1] or last, without requiring the use of the len () function.

The other operators such as concatenate (+) or repeat (*) strings are applicable to any sequence of data,

```
>>> s1 = 'house'
>>> s2 = s1 + 'big'
>>> s2
'big house'
>>> s3 = 3 * s1 + '!'
>>> s3
'househousehouse!'
```

The in operator is considered a Boolean operator over two strings and returns True if the string on the left is a segment (or substring) of the one on the right. If it is not, it returns False. The not in operator returns the opposite logical result. Examples:

```
>>> s = 'wooden house'
>>> 'house' in s
True
>>> 'housewood' in s
False
>>> 'housewood' not in s
True
```

Strings are immutable

Remember that this type of data is considered immutable because we cannot change the values of its elements or change its size. If we want to do that we must create another variable (and another string value before, of course). Let's see, if we want to capitalize the first letter of the string s of the previous example, it gives us an error:

```
>>> s = 'wooden house'
>>> s [0] = 'W'
Traceback (most recent call last):
  File "<stdin>", line 1, in <module>
TypeError: 'str' object does not support item assignment
```

This action of capitalizing the first letter of the string can be done automatically, as shown in the following section, but by creating a new variable.

String methods Python is an object-oriented language and the data in Python is in the objects. In object-oriented programming, objects have associated methods to manipulate their data. The methods are similar to the functions since they receive arguments and return values. Strings have methods that are their own. For example, the upper method takes a string and returns another string but with the uppercase letters.

The upper method instead of being applied to the string s = 'wooden house', as a function, upper (s), is applied in the form s.upper (). That is, a method is applied to its values. Let's look at several methods of the strings (there are methods with and without arguments):

```
>>> s = 'wooden house'
>>> sM = s.upper () # converts the letters to
```

```
uppercase
>>> sM
'WOODEN HOUSE'
>>> sM.lower () # converts the letters to lowercase
'wooden house'
>>> s.capitalize () # first letter of the string in
uppercase
'Wooden house'
>>> s.title () # first letter of each string word in
uppercase
'Wooden House'
>>> i = s.find ('e') # searches the index (position)
of the first string 'e'
>>> i # if it doesn't find the string it returns -1
5
>>> s.count ('a') # count how many times the element
or string appears
0
>>> s.replace ('o', 'e') # replace the first string
with the second
'weeden heuse'
>>> s.split ('') # part s using the string ''
producing list
['wooden', 'house']
>>> s1 = 'Hello'
>>> s1.isupper () # True if all characters in S are
uppercase
False # False otherwise
>>> s1 [0].isupper ()
True
>>> s1.islower () # True if all characters in S are
lowercase
False # False otherwise
```

```
>>> s1 [1].islower ()
True
```

The above code shows a group of typical methods of string values. We solved the problem of capitalizing the first letter with the capitalize () method. The split method divides the string into segments according to the delimiter used as an argument, which in this case is the blank space. The argument " is the default argument, so s. split () can be used to separate words in a text. The resulting substring (words, in this case) is returned in a list with the substring as elements.

Examples

We will show a couple of examples of travel or search in a string to (i) count the number of 'to', (ii) the number of the given character or sub-string 'c_1' and search for a character or substring.

```
def count (s):
  "" "Count letter a in a string
  >>> countLetter ('hot potato', 'a')
  1
  >>> countLetter ('Esplugues', 'a')
  0
  " " "
  n = 0
  for c in s:
       if c == 'a':
       n = n + 1
  return n
```

Option with s.count () method

```
def count (s):
  return s.count ('a')
```

```
def count (s, c1):
  "" "Count letter or sub-string c1 in string s
  Examples:
  >>> count ('hot potato', 'a')
  1
  >>> count ('potato', 'u')
  0
  "" "
  n = 0
  for c in s:
      if c == c1:
      n = n + 1
  return n
```

The search for a character or substring in a string can be done with the structures for, while or directly with some method of the strings. Let's look first at the classic search options with for and while.

```
def search (s, c1):
  "" "search for letter c1 in string s

>>> search ('hot potato', 'a')
  True
>>> search ('potato', 'u')
  False
  "" "
```

```
    OK = False
    for c in s:
            if c == c1:
                OK = True
                Break
    return Ok
```

```
def search (s, c1):
    """search for letter c1 in string s
    Examples:
    >>> search ('hot potato', 'a')
    True
    >>> search ('potato', 'u')
    False
    """
    OK = False
    N = len (s)
    i = 0
    while i <N and not OK:
            if s [i] == c1:
                OK = True
            i + = 1
    return OK
```

In Python we can exit the function within a loop, so the search can be:

```
def search (s, c1):
    """search for letter c1 in string s
    Examples:
    >>> search ('hot potato', 'a')
    True
    >>> search ('potato', 'u')
```

```
        False
    """
    for c in s:
        if c == c1:
            return True
    return False
```

But this search can be done with the methods count (), find () or simply with the Boolean operator in:

```
def search (s, c1):
    """search for letter c1 in string s
    Examples:
    >>> search ('hot potato', 'a')
    True
    >>> search ('potato', 'u')
    False
    """
    return c1 in s
    #return s.count (c1)> 0
    #return s.find (c1)> = 0
```

Tuples

Tuples, like strings, are a sequence of elements arranged in a Python object. Unlike strings (elements are characters) tuples can contain elements of any type, including elements of different types. The elements are indexed the same as the strings, through an integer. The syntax of tuples is a sequence of values separated by commas. Although they are not necessary, they are usually enclosed in parentheses,

```
# Example of tuples
>>> a = 1, 2, 3
>>> to
(1, 2, 3)
>>> b = (3, 4, 5, 'a')
>>> b
(3, 4, 5, 'a')
>>> type (a)
<class 'tuple'>
>>> type (b)
<class 'tuple'>
```

The objects assigned to variables a and b are tuples type. The important thing is to include commas between the elements. For example,

```
>>> t = 'k',
>>> t
('k',)
>>> type (t)
<class 'tuple'>
>>> t2 = 'k'
>>> t2
'k'
>>> type (t2)
<class 'str'>
```

The object 'k' is a tuple, however 'k' is a string. An empty tuple can be created using parentheses without including anything: (). We can also use the internal tuple () function to convert an iterable sequence, such as a string or list, to tuple, or create an empty tuple:

```
>>> tuple ('Hello')
```

```
('H', 'e', 'l', 'l', 'o')
>>> tuple ([1, 2])
(1, 2)
>>> tuple ()
()
```

Indexing, trimming and other tuple operations

Access to tuple elements, element extraction and operations are performed analogously to strings. Let's look at several examples:

```
>>> b = (3, 4, 5, 'a')
>>> b [0]
3
>>> b [-1]
'to'
>>> b [0: 3]
(3. 4. 5)
>>> t = ('the', 'tuples', 'are', 'immutable')
>>> t [0]
'the'
>>> t [1] = 'lists'
Traceback (most recent call last):
  File "<stdin>", line 1, in <module>
TypeError: 'tuple' object does not support item assignment
```

The static or immutable characteristic of the tuples is observed, as are the strings. We can include tuples within tuples and concatenate and repeat them, such as string,

```
>>> b = (3, 4, 5, 'a')
>>> c = (b, 2)
>>> b + c
(3, 4, 5, 'a', (3, 4, 5, 'a'), 2)
>>> 3*b
(3, 4, 5, 'a', 3, 4, 5, 'a', 3, 4, 5, 'a')
```

The iterative Python for - in composition can use any iterable sequence, including tuples:

```
>>> games = ('tennis', 'baseball', 'football', 'volleyball', 'swimming')
>>> for sport in games:
... print (sport)
tennis
baseball
football
volleyball
swimming
```

Also, as in string sequences, in tuples, you can use the operations to concatenate (+) and repeat (*) tuples and the in and not in operators of membership of elements in tuples.

Multiple assignments and functions with multiple returns

Python allows multiple assignments through tuple assignments. These actions allow a tuple of variables to the left of an assignment is assigned a tuple of values to the right of it. The condition to be fulfilled is that the number of variables of the variable tuple is equal to the number of elements of the tuple of values. Even, the object to be assigned multiple times to the variable tuple can be a string or a list, as long as the number of characters or elements is equal to the number of variables in the tuple to which the values are assigned. Let's see some examples

```
>>> a,b,c = (1,2,3)
>>> a
1
>>> type(a)
<class 'int'>
>>> d,e,f = 'xyz'
>>> d
'x'
>>> type(d)
<class 'str'>
```

In the first tuple of variables (a, b, c) the variables receive integer values. Although this object is structured type, tuple, its elements are variables of integer type. Similarly, the tuple of variables (d, e, f) each receives values of type string and its variables will be type string.

This feature of tuple assignments allows solving easily the typical problem of variable exchange, without requiring an auxiliary variable. For example, if we want to exchange the values of the variables x = 5 and y = 7, in the classical languages it would be done:

```
>>> x = 5
>>> y = 7
>>> temp = x # use of auxiliary (temporary) variable
```

```
temp
>>> x = y
>>> y = temp
>>> print (x, y)
7      5
```

With multiple assignments of tuples, the solution is direct:

```
>>> x = 5
>>> y = 7
>>> x, y = y, x
>>> print (x, y)
7      5
```

In the case of functions, they can also return multiple results that can be assigned to multiple variables with the use of tuples. Being strict, functions only return one result. But if that value is a tuple, then it can be assigned to a tuple of variables. The number of elements is required to match. Let's look at the following function as an example:

```
def myFunction (x):
    """
    Returns 2 values: x increased and decreased by 1
    """
        return x + 1, x - 1
a, b = myFunction (10)
print (a, b)
print (myFunction (20))
```

```
>>>
11   9
(21, 19)
```

The function returns a tuple of two values. In the first instruction of the main body of the program these values are assigned to the tuple with the variables a and b. Each of these variables is of the integer type and, for argument 10 of the function, they receive the values 11 and 9, respectively. These values are shown by the first print (). The second print () directly shows the tuple that the function returns.

Functions with an arbitrary number of parameters, using tuples

In the previous topic, we analyzed functions with keywords arguments. There is the option to define a function with an arbitrary (variable) number of parameters using the * operator before the parameter name. Let's look at the function of the following example and its different calls.

```
def mean (* pair):
    sum = 0
    for elem in pair:
    sum = sum + elem
    return sum / len (pair)
print (average (3, 4))
print (average (10.2, 14, 12, 9.5, 13.4, 8, 9.2))
print (average (2))
```

```
>>>
3.5
```

```
10.9
2.0
```

The function calculates the average value of the sequence of numbers that is sent as an argument to the input parameter, which expects to receive a tuple. The function can be improved to avoid dividing by 0, in case of entering an empty tuple.

Tuple Methods

As in the strings, there are methods associated with tuple type objects and lists. but only the methods: s.index (x) and s.count (x). You can also use the internal functions max and min when the tuples (or lists) are of numerical values. If the elements are strings, calculate the major or minor element, according to the position in the ASCII table of the first character. Let's see some examples,

```
a = (2, 3, 4, 5, 79, -8, 5, -4)
>>> a.index (5) # index of the first occurrence of 5 in a
3
>>> a.count (5) # total occurrences of 5 in a
2
>>> max
79
>>> min (a)
-8
>>> b = ('az', 'b', 'x')
>>> max (b)
'x'
>>> min (b)
'az'
```

Zip function

It is an iterator that operates on several iterable ones and creates tuples by adding elements of the iterable sequences (string, tuples, lists, etc.).

Example

```
def AccountElemsSamePosition(s1, s2):
    "" "tell how many equal letters are in the same
position in 2
    S1 and S2 words. You can use lists or tuples
    >>> AccountElemsSamePosition ('Hello', 'Casting')
    3
    "" "
    counter = 0
  for c1, c2, in zip (s1, s2):
            if c1 == c2:
                counter + = 1
    return counter
```

```
>>> AccountElemsSamePosition ('Hello', 'Goodbye')
0
>>> AccountElemsSamePosition ('Hello', 'Casting')
3
```

Frozen sets (Frozen set)

In Python, there is another group of heterogeneous structured data that try to keep a certain relationship with set theory. These data are the Set and Frozen set sets. The first ones are presented in the following section of structured mutable or dynamic data.

A frozen set (Frozen set) is a collection of unordered items that are unique and immutable. That is, it can contain numbers, string, tuples, but not lists. That they are unique elements means that they are not repeated. The Set and Frozen set are not sequences of data.

Frozen sets are immutable because they cannot be changed or removed or added. Examples of frozen data:

```
>>> FS1 = frozenset ({25, 4, 'a', 2, 25, 'house', 'a'})
>>> FS1
frozenset ({2, 'a', 4, 'house', 25})
>>> type (FS1)
<class 'frozenset'>
>>> len (FS1)
5
```

The repeated elements (25 and 'a') that we included in the frozen set were discarded.

Types of structured mutable (dynamic) data

Unlike the frozen strings, tuples and sets, the structured mutable data, also called dynamic, are characterized in that their elements can change in value and elements can be added or deleted.

In Python, we have as mutable structured data the lists, the sets (Set) and the dictionaries. The lists and sets (Set) can be considered as the mutable equivalents to the frozen tuples and sets (Frozenset), respectively.

Lists

The lists, as well as tuples and strings, are formed by a sequence of data. But unlike tuples, its elements can be modified, eliminated or increased. The elements of the lists can be simple data (numerical or Boolean), strings, tuples or other lists. Elements are indexed the same as tuples and string, through an integer. The syntax of the lists is a sequence of comma-separated values enclosed in square brackets.

Example

```
>>> v1 = [2, 4, 6, 8, 10]
>>> type (v1)
<class 'list'>
>>> v2 = [7, 8.5, 'a', 'Hello', (2, 3), [11, 12]]
>>> v2
[7, 8, 'a', 'Hello', (2, 3), [11, 12]]
>>> games = ['tennis', 'baseball', 'football', 'volleyball', 'swimming']
>>> games
['tennis', 'baseball', 'football', 'volleyball', 'swimming']
```

The v1 list consists of integers, while v2 includes integers, real numbers, strings, tuples and a list as its last element. The variable games refer to a list object with 5 elements of type string. It is similar to the previously defined tuple, but its elements can be modifiable. It is a dynamic structure.

We can generate a list with a sequence of integers with the data type range (), of the form,

```
>>> v = list (range (1,11))
>>> v
[1, 2, 3, 4, 5, 6, 7, 8, 9, 10]
```

In Python versions 2.x, range () is a function that directly generates a list. However, in versions 3.x, being range () a type of data range, we have to convert it to a list with the function list (). This function also serves to convert iterable data types, such as strings or tuples to list type. You can also create an empty list. Examples:

```
>>> t = (1, 2, 3)
>>> list (t)
[1, 2, 3]
>>> s = 'Hello'
>>> list (s)
['Hi']
>>> e = list () # empty list
>>> e = [] # empty list
```

Indexing, trimming and other list operations

In the lists, access to its elements, the extraction of elements and operations are carried out in the same way as in strings and tuples. The slice operators [n: m] are also used in the lists. Let's look at several examples:

```
>>> v2 = [7, 8, 'a', 'Hello', (2,3), [11, 12]]
>>> v2 [0]
7
>>> v2 [-1]
[11, 12]
```

```
>>> v2 [-2]
(2. 3)
>>> v2 [0: 3]
[7, 8, 'a']
>>> t = ['las', 'lists', 'are', 'mutable']
>>> t [3] = 'dynamic'
>>> t
['the', 'lists', 'are', 'dynamic']
>>> len (t)
4
```

The mutability of the lists can be observed. Lists can be concatenated and repeated with the + and * operators, respectively, such as strings and tuples,

```
>>> v1 = [2, 4, 6, 8, 10]
>>> v3 = [3, 5, 7]
>>> v1 + v3
[2, 4, 6, 8, 10, 3, 5, 7]
>>> 3*v3
[3, 5, 7, 3, 5, 7, 3, 5, 7]
```

The iterative Python for - in composition has already been used with lists in the subject of iterative compositions. With the previously defined games list, we get:

```
>>> for sport in games:
...     print (sport)
tennis
baseball
football
```

```
volleyball
swimming
```

In addition, as in the string and tuple sequences, the lists can be concatenated with the + operator and repeated with the * operator. Boolean operators in and not in, as in strings and tuples, evaluate whether or not an element belongs to a sequence (string, tuple or list). Examples

```
>>> v2 = [7, 8, 'a', 'Hello', (2,3), [11, 12]]
>>> 8 in v2
True
>>> 'Hello' in v2
True
>>> 'HELLO' not in v2
True
```

Objects, values and references

The operator 'id' is available in Python. It indicates whether two variables are referred to the same object or not. Executing the instructions, we have:

```
>>> a = 'house'
>>> b = 'house'
>>> id (a)
123917904
>>> id (b)
123917904
>>> a is b
True
```

You can see that both variables a and b are referred to the same object, which has a 'house' value and occupies the memory position 123917904 (this position is arbitrary). The instruction "a is b" is true.

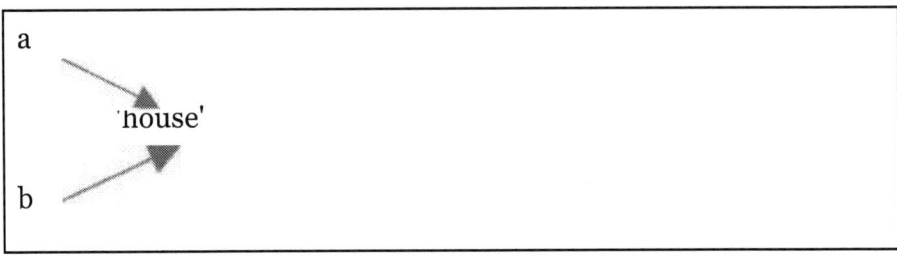

In string data types, being immutable, Python creates only one object per memory economy and both variables are referred to the same object. However, with the lists, being mutable, although two lists with the same values are formed, Python creates two objects, which occupy different memory locations:

```
>>> a = [1, 2, 3]
>>> b = [1, 2, 3]
>>> id(a)
123921992
>>> id(b)
123923656
>>> a is b
False
```

```
────▶a
[1, 2, 3]
────▶b
[1, 2, 3]
```

The lists assigned to variables a and b, although with the same value, are different objects. But you have to be careful with the variable assignments to the same mutable object. In the following example, when copying a variable, no other object is created, but copying refers to the same object:

```
>>> a = [1, 2, 3]
>>> b = a
>>> id(b) # a and b --> [1, 2, 3]
123921992
>>> a is b
True
```

It can be said that the variable b is an alias of a and that they are referenced. Therefore, if we modify or add a value to the object [1, 2, 3], through one of the variables, then we modify the other. Let's see

```
>>> b[0] = 15
>>> a
[15, 2, 3]
```

This effect can give unexpected results if not handled carefully. However, this property is used to pass parameters by reference in functions that behave as a procedure. If we want to copy one variable from another, we have the copy method, which will be presented below.

Object-oriented programming with Python

Python allows several programming paradigms, including object-oriented programming (OOP). The OOP is a way of structuring the code that makes it especially effective by organizing and reusing code, although its abstract nature makes it not very intuitive when it starts.

Object-oriented programming in Python is optional and so far, we have not used it directly, although indirectly we have done so from the beginning. Although its biggest advantage appears with long and more complex programs, it is very useful to understand how POO works since this is how Python works internally.

The basic idea is simple. If we have a more complex type of data than we have seen so far as lists or dictionaries and we want to create a new type of data with particular properties, we can define it with a class, something similar to a def function. Suppose we want to create a type of data called Star (Star), which to begin with will only have one name, we can write:

```
# Let's create star.py
class Star(object):
    """Class for stars"""
    def __init__(self, name):
        self.name = name
    # Special method called when doing print
    def __str__(self):
        return "Stars {}".format(self.name)
```

The class has a special main function __init__ () that builds the element of the Star class (called an object) and is executed when it creates a new object or instance of that class; we have put name as the only mandatory parameter, but it does not have to have any.

The mysterious self-variable with which each function begins (called methods on objects), refers to the specific object we are creating, this will be clearer with an example. Now we can create Star type objects:

```
# Star.py library that includes the Star import star
class
# New instance (object) of Star, with a parameter (the
name), mandatory star1 = star.Star («Altair»)
# What returns when printing the object, according to
the method __str__ print (star1) # Star Altair
print (star1.name) # Altair
```

When creating the object with name star1, which in the class definition we call self, we have a new data type with the name property. Now we can add some methods that can be applied to the Star object:

```
class Star:
    "" "Star class
    Example classes with Python
    File: star.py

    "" "
    # Total number of stars
    num_stars = 0
    def __init__ (self, name):
        self.name = name
        Star.num_stars + = 1
    def set_mag (self, mag):
        self.mag = mag
    def set_pair (self, pair):
        "" "Assigns parallax in arc seconds" ""
        self.pair = pair
```

```
    def get_mag (self):
        print "The magnitude of {} of {}". format
(self.name, self.mag)
    def get_dist (self):
        "" "Calculate the distance in parsec from the
parallax" ""
        print "The distance of {} is {: .2f} pc"
.format (self.name, 1 / self.par)
    def get_stars_number (self):
        print "Total number of stars: {}". format
(Star.num_stars)
```

Now we can do more things a Star object:

```
import star
# I create a star instance
altair = star.Star ('Altair')
altair.name
# Returns 'Altair'
altair.set_pair (0.195)
altair.get_stars_number ()
# Returns: Total number of stars: 1
# I use a general class method
star.pc2ly (5.13)
# Returns: 16.73406
altair.get_dist ()
# Returns: The distance of Altair is 5.13 pc
# I create another star instance
other = star.Star ('Vega')
otro.get_stars_number ()
# Returns: Total number of stars: 2
altair.get_stars_number ()
```

```
# Returns: Total number of stars: 2
```

Is not all this familiar? It is similar to the methods and properties of Python elements such as strings or lists, which are also objects defined in classes with their methods.

Objects have an interesting property called inheritance that allows you to reuse properties of other objects. Suppose we are interested in a particular type of star called a white dwarf, which are Star stars with some special properties, so we will need all the properties of the Star object and some new ones that we will add:

```
class WBStar (Star):
    "" "Class for White Dwarfs (WD)" ""
    def __init__ (self, name, type):
        "" "WD type: dA, dB, dC, dO, dZ, dQ" ""
        self.name = name
        self.type = type
        Star.num_stars + = 1
    def get_type (self):
        return self.type
    def __str__ (self):
        return "White Dwarf {} of type {}". format (self.name, self.type)
```

Now, as a class parameter, instead of using an object to create a new object, we have set Star to inherit the properties of that class. Thus, when creating a WDStar object we are creating a different object, with all the Star properties and methods and a new property called type. We also overwrite the result when printing with print defining the special method __str__.

As we can see, the methods, which are the functions associated with the objects, only apply to them. If in our file the class, which we have called star.py and that now contains the Star and WDStar classes, we add a normal function, this can be used as usual:

```
class Star (Star):
    ...
class WBStar (Star):
    ...
def pc2ly (dist):
    "" "Converts parsec to many years" ""
    return dist * 3,262
And as always:
import star
# Convert parsecs into light years
distance_ly = Star.pc2ly (10.0)
```

Data Science Algorithms and Models

This guidebook has taken some time to look through a lot of the different parts that come with data analysis. We took a look at what data analysis is all about, how to work with the Python language and why it is such a good thing for the data analysis, and even some of the basics of Machine Learning and why this should be a part of our process.

With all of this in mind, it is now time for us to move on to some of the other things that we can do when working on this process. We are going to explore some of the best algorithms and models that we can use to complete our data analysis with the help of the Python language. There are so many different algorithms that we can choose from, and all of them are going to be great options to get the work done. With this in mind, let's dive right in and see what some of the best algorithms and models are for completing your business data analysis with Python.

Neural Networks

It is hard to have a discussion about Machine Learning and data analysis without taking some time to talk about neural networks and how these forms of coding are meant to work. Neural networks are a great addition to any Machine Learning model because they can work similarly to the human brain. When they get the answer right, they can learn from that, and some of the synapses that bring it all together will get stronger. The more times that this algorithm can get an answer right, the faster and more efficient it can become with its job as well.

With neural networks, each of the layers that you go through will spend a bit of time at that location, seeing if there is any pattern. This is often done with images or videos so it will go through each layer of that image and see whether or not it can find a new pattern. If the network does find one of these patterns, then it is going to instigate the process that it needs to move over to the following layer. This is a process that continues, with the neural network going through many layers until the algorithm has created a good idea of what the image is and can give an accurate prediction.

There are then going to be a few different parts that can show up when we reach this point, and it depends on how the program is set up to work. If the algorithm was able to go through the process above and could sort through all of the different layers, then it is going to make a prediction. If the prediction it provides is right, the neurons in the system will turn out stronger than ever. This is because the program is going to work with artificial intelligence to make the stronger connections and associations that we need to keep this process going. The more times that our neural network can come back with the correct answer, the more efficient this neural network will become in the future when we use it.

If the program has been set up properly, it is going to make the right prediction that there is a car in the picture. The program can come up with this prediction based on some of the features that it already knows belongs to the car, including the color, the number on the license plate, the placement of the doors, the headlights, and more.

When you are working with some of the available conventional coding methods, this process can be really difficult to do. You will find that the neural network system can make this a really easy system to work with.

For the algorithm to work, you would need to provide the system with an image of the car. The neural network would then be able to look over the picture. It would start with the first layer, which would be the outside edges of the car. Then it would go through some other layers that help the neural network understand if any unique characteristics are present in the picture that outlines that it is a car. If the program is good at doing the job, it is going to get better at finding some of the smallest details of the car, including things like its windows and even wheel patterns.

There could potentially be a lot of different layers that come with this one, but the more layers and details that the neural network can find, the more accurately it will be able to predict what kind of car is in front of it. If your neural network is accurate in identifying the car model, it is going to learn from this lesson. It will remember some of these patterns and characteristics that showed up in the car model and will store them for use later. The next time that they encounter the same kind of car model, they will be able to make a prediction pretty quickly.

When working with this algorithm, you are often going to choose one and use it, when you want to go through a large number of pictures and find some of the defining features that are inside of them. For example, there is often a big use for this kind of thing when you are working with face recognition software. All of the information wouldn't be available ahead of time with this method. And you can teach the computer how to recognize the right faces using this method instead. It is also one that is highly effective when you want it to recognize different animals, define the car models, and more.

As you can imagine, there are several advantages that we can see when we work with this kind of algorithm. One of these is that we can work with this method, and we won't have to worry as much about the statistics that come with it. Even if you need to work with the algorithm and you don't know the statistics or don't have them available, the neural network can be a great option to work with to ensure that any complex relationship will show up.

Naïve Bayes

We can also work with an algorithm that is known as the Naïve Bayes algorithm. This is a great algorithm to use any time that you have people who want to see some more of the information that you are working on, and who would like to get more involved in the process, but they are uncertain about how to do this, and may not understand the full extent of what you are doing. It is also helpful if they want to see these results before the algorithm is all the way done.

As you work through some of the other algorithms on this page and see what options are available for handling the data, you will notice that they often take on hundreds of thousands of points of data. This is why it takes some time to train and test the data, and it can be frustrating for those on the outside to find out they need to wait before they can learn anything about the process. Showing information to the people who make the decisions and the key shareholders can be a challenge when you are just getting started with the whole process.

This is where the Naïve Bayes algorithm comes in. It is able to simplify some of the work that you are doing. It will usually not be the final algorithm that you use, but it can often give a good idea to others outside of the process about what you are doing. It can answer questions, puts the work that you are doing in a much easier to understand the form, and can make sure that everyone will be on the same page.

Clustering Algorithms

One of the best types of algorithms that you can work with is going to be the clustering algorithm. There are a variety of clustering algorithms out there to focus on, but they are going to help us ensure that the program can learn something on its own, and will be able to handle separating the different data points that we have. These clustering algorithms work best when you can keep things simple. It takes some of the data that you are working with and then makes some clusters that come together. Before we start with the program though, we can choose the number of clusters that we want to fit the information too.

The number of clusters that you go with is going to depend on what kind of information you are working with as well. If you just want to separate your customers by gender, then you can work with just two clusters. If you would like to separate the customers by their age or some other feature, then you may need some more clusters to get this done. You can choose the number of clusters that you would like to work with.

The nice thing that comes with the clustering algorithms is that they will handle most of the work of separating and understanding the data for you. This is because the algorithm is in charge of how many points of data go into each of the clusters you choose, whether there are two clusters or twenty that you want to work with. When you take a look at one of these clusters, you will notice that with all of the points inside it is safe to assume that these data points are similar or share something important. This is why they fell into the same cluster with one another.

Once we can form some of these original clusters, it is possible to take each of the individual ones and divide them up to get some more sets of clusters because this can sometimes provide us with more insights. We can do this a few times, which helps to create more division as we go through the steps. In fact, it is possible to go through these iterations enough times that the centroids will no longer change. This is a sign that it is time to be done with the process.

Support Vector Machines

Another option that we need to work with is known as the support vector machine or SVM. When we work with this one, it is important to take all of the items in our data set, and then work on plotting them into one n-dimensional space, rather than having them all over the place. N is going to be the number of features that should show up in this algorithm along with the rest of our information. We then have the option to take the value of all these features and translate them over to the value that is in your coordinates. From here, we determine where the hyperplane is because this will show us the differences that are there between our various classes.

You may notice while working on this kind of algorithm that more than one support vector is going to show up. Many of these are easy to ignore because they are just the coordinates of individual observations that are seen. You can then use the SVM as a frontier that can separate them into classes. The two support vectors that we need to focus on will be the hyperplane and the line.

To do this, we need to make sure that we know where the hyperplane is. as we go through this process, there can sometimes be more than one hyperplane to pick from depending on the kind of data we are working with. There can also be an additional challenge because we want to ensure that with these options, we go with the one that helps us to understand the data, not one that leads us astray. The good thing to consider here is that even if you do see more than one option to work with, there are a few steps that you can follow to make it easier to pick the right one. The steps that you can follow to make this happen will include:

- We are going to start with three hyperplanes that we will call 1, 2, and 3. Then we are going to spend time figuring out which hyperplane is right so that we can classify the star and the circle.

- The good news is there is a pretty simple rule that you can follow so that it becomes easier to identify which hyperplane is the right one. The hyperplane that you want to go with will be the one that segregates your classes the best.

- That one was easy to work with, but in the next one, our hyperplanes of 1, 2, and 3 are all going through the classes and they similarly segregate them. For example, all of the lines or these hyperplanes are going to run parallel with each other. From here you may find that it is hard to pick which hyperplane is the right one.

- For the above issue, we will need to use what is known as the margin. This is the distance that occurs between the hyperplane and the nearest data point from either of the two classes. Then you will be able to get some numbers that can help you out. These numbers may be closer together, but they will point out which hyperplane is going to be the best.

With the example that we have above, we see one of the times that this is a great tool to work within Machine Learning. When we look through some of the points of data that are available, and if you notice that there is a pretty good margin that separates some of the points, then this is a good place to work with the SVM model. It is effective and it can help us find some of the results that we want in the process as well.

Decision Trees

Decisions trees are also a good option that we can work with when we want to take a few available options, and then compare them to see what the possible outcome of each option is all about. We can even combine a few of these decision trees to make a random forest and get more results and predictions from this.

The decision tree is going to be one of the best ways to compare a lot of options, and then choose the path that is going to be the best for your needs. Sometimes there are a whole host of options that we can choose from, and many times they will all seem like great ideas. For businesses who need to choose from the best option out of the group, and need to know which one is likely to give them the results that they are looking for, the decision tree is the best option.

With the decision tree, we can place the data we have into it, and then see the likely outcome that is going to result from making a certain decision. This prediction can help us to make smart business decisions based on what we see. If we had a few different options with this and compare the likely outcomes from each one, it is much easier to determine which course of action is the best one for us to take.

K-Nearest Neighbors

The next algorithm that we can look at is known as the K-Nearest Neighbors algorithm or KNN. When we work with this algorithm, the goal is to search through all of the data that we have for the k most similar example of any instance that we want to work with. Once we can complete this process, then the algorithm can move on to the next step, which is where it will look through all of the information that you have and provide you with a summary. Then the algorithm will take those results and give you some of the predictions you need to make good business decisions.

With this learning algorithm, you will notice that the learning you are working with becomes more competitive. This works to your advantage because there will be a big competition going on between the different elements or the different parts in the models so that you can get the best solution or prediction based on the data you have at hand.

There are several benefits that we can receive when it comes to working with this algorithm. For example, it is a great one that cuts through all of that noise that sometimes shows up in our data. This noise, depending on the set of data that you use, can be really loud, and cutting this down a bit can help make a big difference in the insights that you can see.

And if you are trying to handle and then go through some of the larger amounts of data that some companies have all at once, then this is a great algorithm to go with as well. Unlike some of the others that need to limit the set of data by a bit, the KNN algorithm is going to be able to handle all of your data, no matter how big the set is. Keep in mind that sometimes the computational costs are going to be higher with this kind of method, but in some cases, this is not such a big deal to work with.

To make the K-Nearest neighbors algorithm work the way that you want, there are going to be a few steps that will make this process a little bit easier.

Working with this algorithm can help us to get a lot done when it is time to work with putting parts together, and seeing where all of our data are meant to lie. If you follow the steps that we have above, you will be able to complete this model for yourself, and see some of the great results in the process when it is time to make predictions and good business decisions.

The Markov Algorithm

Another type of unsupervised Machine Learning algorithm that you can work with is the Markov algorithm. This particular algorithm is going to take the data that you decide to input into it, and then it will translate it to help work in another coding language if you choose. The nice thing here is that you can pick out which rules you want to use with this algorithm ahead of time so that the algorithm will work the way that you want. Many programmers in Machine Learning find that this algorithm, and the fact they can set up their own rules ahead of time, is nice because it allows you to take a string of data and ensure that it is as useful as possible as you learn on the job and figure out the parameters of how the data will behave.

Another thing that you may like about this Markov algorithm is that you can work with it in several ways, rather than being stuck with just one method. One option to consider here is that this algorithm works well with things like DNA. For example, you could take the DNA sequence of someone, and then use this algorithm to translate the information that is inside that sequence into some numerical values. This can often make it easier for programmers, doctors, and scientists and more to know what information is present, and to make better predictions into the future. When you are working with programmers and computers, you will find that the numerical data are going to be much easier to sort through than other options of looking through DNA.

A good reason why you would need to use the Markov algorithm is that it is great at learning problems when you already know the input you want to use, but you are not sure about the parameters. This algorithm is going to be able to find insights that are inside of the information. In some cases, these insights are hidden and this makes it hard for the other algorithms we have discussed to find them.

There are still some downfalls to working with the Markov algorithm. This one can sometimes be difficult to work with because you do need to manually go through and create a new rule any time that you want to bring in a new programming language. If you only want to work with one type of programming language on your project, then this is not going to be a big deal. But many times, your program will need to work with several different languages, and going in and making the new rules a bunch of times can get tedious.

Regression Analysis (Linear Regression and Logistic Regression)

Several industries across the globe are struggling with the best way to come up with the correct data or information that will eventually enable them to solve their incurring prediction problems. Several banks have made some losses, especially within their credit section as they could not correctly predict the trustfulness of the defaulters. In the health sector, you realize many have lost their lives because of poor planning and risk management, which come as a result of the lack of modeling to tool for more straightforward prediction. We also have other sectors such as weather forecasting where farmers were not advised on the occurrence of rain, as a result leading to more losses. Another area involved the payment of mortgage by homeowners. Due to all these, everyone across the universe went on a rampage looking for the best possible way to handle the prediction roles of the organizations. Later on, all these gave birth to what is termed as regression analysis.

Therefore, regression analysis refers to statistical processes for prediction analysis using variables. In that, it helps in identifying the variables relationships. This analysis consists of both independent and dependent variables. In other words, regression analysis aids in understanding the effect of one independent variable on the dependent variable when other independent variables are kept constant. In most cases, regression analysis will try hard to predict the conditional expectation, especially of the dependent variable.

Regression analysis is applied in several areas such as weather forecasting and prediction. Here, it helps predict the outcome of the rain within a specific period. It is also applicable in other fields such as medical sectors for predicting the chances of diseases. Regression analysis comprises of the following: linear regression, logistic regression, polynomial, stepwise, ridge, lasso, and elastic net regression. All in all, this chapter will only tackle the most widely used regression analysis, such as linear regression and logistic regression. It is good to note that ElasticNet regression is a combination of the Lasso and Ridge regression.

Linear Regression

Linear regression refers to a statistical approach used for modeling a relationship between various variables in a particular set of different independent variables. In this chapter, you'll learn more about dependent variables such as response as well as independent variables, including features of simplicity. To be able to offer extensive search results and have a clear understanding of linear regression in Python, you need to be keen on a primary basis. We begin with the primary version of the subject. For instance, what is a simple linear regression?

By definition, simple linear regression refers to a significant approach that's used in predicting a significant response by utilizing a single feature. Therefore, it's assumed that the main two variables, in this case, are directly related. That's why it's vital to determine the linear function since it often predicts the main response value of the equation accurately. There are different regression models utilized in showing as well as predicting the main relationship between two different variables as well as factors. As such, it's important to note that the main factor that's being predicted is known as the dependent variable. But the factors utilized in predicting the main value of the dependent variable is identified as the independent variable. With that said, it's also vital to note that good data doesn't always narrate the entire story as it may be. Therefore, regression analysis is often used in the research as well as the establishment of the correlation of variables. However, correlation isn't the same as the subject of causation. Therefore, a line found in a simple linear regression that may be fitting into the data points appropriately may not indicate a definitive element regarding a major cause and effect relationship. When it comes to linear regression, every observation has two values. Therefore, one of the values is specifically for the dependent variable. The other is certainly for the independent variable.

Linear Regression in Python

When discussing the simple linear regression analysis, we are looking at some of the simplest forms of regression analysis that are used on various independent variables as well as one independent variable.

Consequently, in such a model, a straight line is often used in approximating the main relationship between an independent as well as a dependent variable. Multiple regression analysis occurs when there are 2 major independent variables applied in regression analysis. As a result, the model is not going to be a slightly simple linear one. Usually, this model (y= β_0 +β_1 + E.) represents simple linear regression.

By applying the relevant mathematical convention, two main factors are herein involved. They include x and y which are the main designations. Also, the equation often describes how y correlates with x. This is what is defined as the regression model. Apart from that, the linear regression model has an error term which is often represented by E. It can also be termed as the Greek letter epsilon. Usually, this error term is applied to mainly account for the variability found in y. However, this element cannot be explained in terms of the linear relationship found between x as well as y. It's also important to note that parameters are representing the major population being studied. Some of these parameters represent the main population that is being studied. Usually, a regression line can easily show how a unique positive linear relationship, no relationship, as well as a negative relationship.

With that said, if the line that has been graphed appears to be in a simple linear regression that's flat in any way, no relationship will be found in the two variables. On the other hand, if the regression line slopes upwards with the line's lower end located at y, on the graph, then there will be a positive linear relationship within the graph. But if the regression line tends to slope downward where the upper end of y that intercepts at the graph's axis. In the case where the parameters are well identified and known, the equation of the simple linear regression can utilize the computed meaning of the value of y. But in real practice, various parameter values aren't known. Therefore, they have to be estimated using some forms of data sampling from the actual population. Therefore, the parameters of these populations are often estimated using sample statistics. These statistics can be represented using $\beta_0 + \beta_1$.

It is clear that we live in a world that requires us to use tons of data coupled with powerful computers as well as artificial intelligence. While this may only be the beginning, there is a rise in the use of Data Science in various sectors across the world. Machine learning is also driving image recognition as well as autonomous vehicles development and decisions based in the sector of finance as well as the energy industry.

As such, linear regression in Python is still a fundamental statistical as well as Machine Learning technique. Therefore, for those who aspire to do statistics or scientific computing, there are high chances that this will be a requirement in the course work. Not only it is advisable to indulge in the learning process but also proceed to various complex methods appended to the studies.

It's important to understand the different types of linear regression. One of them includes multiple linear regressions that involve a unique case of the linear regression that has two to more independent variables. As such, in a case where there are two independent variables, it happens that the probable regression function is going to represent a major regression plane situated in a three-dimensional space. As such, the objective of the regression appears to be the value that will determine different weights. This also happens to be as close to the actual response as possible. In a different scenario, the case that exceeds two independent variables is often similar.

However, it's more general as well. In a similar case, you may regard polynomial regression as a major generalized issue of linear regression in Python. With that said, you can easily assume the polynomial dependence found between the output as well as inputs. In that case, your regression function may also be f which can include other non-linear terms.

Usually, linear regression is the initial Machine Learning algorithm that data scientists encounter in their practice. It's a vital model that everyone in the sector should master. This is because it helps in laying a strong foundation for different Machine Learning algorithms. For starters, it may be utilized in forecasting sales by analyzing sales data for initial months. Also, it may be used in gaining important insight regarding consumer behavior.

Logistic Regression

Logistic regression comprises of logistic model, logistic function, statistics model, and much more. Therefore, many organizations apply logistic regression in their day to day activities which mainly composed of data predictions and analysis. You can always conduct this regression analysis, especially when the dependent variable is binary. That's dichotomous.

Just like other types of regression analyses, logistic regression is entirely applied in any analysis dealing with prediction. Its primary function, in this case, is to describe data. Also, logistic regression can be used to explain or illustrate the kind of relationship between the binary variable, which is the dependent one, and the other variables, which are the independent ones. This regression might look challenging to interpret, but with the help of specific tools such as Intellectus Statistics, you can easily undertake your data analysis.

Logistic regression knowledge can be easily applied in statistics with the help of the logistic model. In this case, the primary function of the logistic model is actually to come up with the correct results of certain predictions or classes with the help of probability. For example, probability works best in areas where you are only required to predict the outcome of the existing events. These events include: healthy or sick, win or lose, alive or dead, or even in places where you are making your analysis about the test where someone either fails or passes. Still, in this model, you will be able to fine-tune your result primarily through probability. In the case of an image, you will be able to extend your model to cover up various classes. You will be able to detect whether the image in your analysis is a lion or a cat, and so on. In this case, the individual variables within the image will have their probability numbers between 0 and 1. However, the sum here should be adding up to one.

Therefore, logistic regression refers to a basic statistical model that makes greater use of the available logistic function regardless of the complexity of more extensions that might exist. Logistic regression is part and parcel of the regression analysis, and on many occasions, it is applied in various analyses where logistic model parameters are estimated. Remember, the logistic model is like a form or a type of binary regression. Therefore, a binary regression consists of a binary logistic model. This model is composed of a dependent variable which includes two possible values of events. These values can be represented as pass/fail, alive/dead, good/bad, and much more. You need to note that the indicator variable actually denotes these possible values and always they have labeled 0 and 1. Within this logistic model, the odds logarithm that's log-odds, for the values of 1 represents a linear combination. In that, this combination has got one or more variables that are entirely independent. In this case, they are called predictors here.

Moreover, in logistic regression analysis, independent variables sometimes may each form a binary variable or sometimes a continuous variable. In the case of a binary variable, there must be the presence of two classes or events, and they have to be coded by the indicator variables. However, on the other hand, continuous variable represents real value. In the logistic regression analysis, the corresponding probability of these values always varies between 0 and 1 as has been denoted previously above. In this analysis, these log-odds, that's, algorithms of odds will be converted by logistic function into probability. Log odds are measured in logit which also a derivative of its name (logistic unit). Again, you can also use a probit model with a different sigmoid function to convert the log odds into a probability for easy analysis. You need to note that the probit model is an example of an analogous model which comprises of the sigmoid function.

All in all, you will realize that the logistic model is the most preferred in this conversion due to its defining attributes or characteristics. One such feature of the logistic model is its ability to increase the multiplicatively scales of each of the independent variables. As a result of this, it produces an outcome with parameters assigned to each independent variable at a constant rate. However, this will generalize the odd ratio if at all, it is part of a variable which is a binary dependent.

It is also good to note that there are extensions when it comes to dependent variables, especially in some regression such as binary logistic. However, this extension is only applicable where two or more levels are used. These two extensions include multinomial logistic regression which works best with categorical outputs, especially the one having several values that's, two values and above. The next type of logistic regression extension is the ordinal logistic regression which deals with a huge collection of multiple categories. A good example here is the ordinal logistic model dealing with the proportional odds. However, this system only does modeling and not performing any classifications dealing with the statistics since it is not a classifier. Therefore, it will only convert the probability input into an output. Following this, let us discuss the applications of logistic regression in a real-life situation.

Applications of Logistic Regression

Logistic regression is applied in metrological and other forecasting stations which consist of meteorologists. The algorithm here is used to predict the probability of rain. This information is vital as it helps in many sectors such as agricultural, transport and so on. Time of planting can efficiently be planned for, and the right arrangement can be put into place.

This analysis is also applied in some risk management systems such as the credit control system. Here, the analysis will predict whether the account holder is a defaulter when it comes to payment or not. Still, on this, the regression analysis will predict the exact amount that someone can be given by using the previous records. This always enables many organizations to run, as they can control everything when it comes to risk management. All accounts will undergo a critical analysis before any credit is appended. Logistic regression is also applied in political sectors, especially during an election. Here, it gives out the probability of winning and losing each candidate owing to their strengths and resources they used. Again, this regression analysis will be able to predict the number of people who might fail to vote and who will vote at the end and to which particular candidate. Some factors help determine the prediction outcome here such as the age of the candidate, sex, the incomes of both the candidate and the voters, state of the residence of both and the total number of votes in the last elections.

Logistic regression is also applied in various medical fields. It is applied in epidemiology. Here, the analysis is used to identify all those risk factors that may eventually result in diseases. As a result, precautions and other preventive measures may be put into place. Its knowledge is usable in the Trauma and Injury Severity Score(TRISS) where predictions of mortality, especially in injured patients, are done. We have several medical scales that have been designed to check on the severity of patients across the globe.

All these medical scales have been developed or managed using logistic regression. In most cases, especially within the health sector, you can use this knowledge to predict the risk of acquiring some dangerous diseases. For example, diseases such as coronary heart disease, diabetes, and other forms of health-related complications can be easily controlled. These predictions are based on the day to day observable characteristics of the individual patient. The traits or characteristics here include the body mass index, sex, age, and even different results of their blood tests. This will eventually help in proper planning and risk management in the medical sector.

Again, this knowledge can be applied in the engineering sector. Here, it is used to predict the failure probability of a particular system, a new product, or even any kind of process. In the field of marketing, logistic regression analysis helps to determine the buyers' purchasing power, their propensity to purchase, and also this knowledge can be used to stop the various subscriptions of the companies. The technique is also applied in economics. Here, knowledge is used to predict the outcome of being involved in the public labor sector. We also have this technique in the issues to do with the probability of homeowners not paying a mortgage. Natural language processing uses conditional random fields which is also an extension of logistic regression, especially to sequential data.

Logistic Regression vs. Linear Regression

You may be wondering about the main difference between these two examples of regressions. In terms of the outcome, linear regression is responsible for the continuous prediction while there is a discrete outcome in logistic regression. A model predicting the price of a car will depend on various parameters like color, year of make, and so on. Therefore, this value will always be different, indicating the continuous outcome. However, a discrete outcome is always one thing. That's, in case of sickness, you can either be sick or not.

Advantages of logistic regression
- It is very effective and efficient

- You can get an outcome without large computational resources
- You can easily interpret it
- No input features required for the scaling process
- No tuning required
- You can easily regularize logistic regression

How Does Machine Learning Compare to AI

One thing that we need to spend some time working on and understanding before we move on is the difference between Artificial Intelligence and Machine learning. Machine learning is going to do a lot of different tasks when we look at the field of Data Science, and it also fits into the category of artificial intelligence at the same time. But we have to understand that Data Science is a pretty broad term, and there are going to be many concepts that will fit into it. One of these concepts that fit under the umbrella of Data Science is Machine Learning, but we will also see other terms that include big data, data mining, and artificial intelligence. Data science is a newer field that is growing more as people find more uses for computers and use these more often.

Another thing that you can focus on when you bring out Data Science is the field of statistics, and it is going to be put together often in Machine Learning. You can work with the focus on classical statistics, even when you are at the higher levels so that the data set will always stay consistent throughout the whole thing. Of course, the different methods that you use to make this happen will depend on the type of data that is put into this and how complex the information that you are using gets as well.

This brings up the question here about the differences that show up between Machine Learning and artificial intelligence and why they are not the same thing. There are a lot of similarities that come with these two options, but the major differences are what sets them apart, and any programmer who wants to work with Machine Learning has to understand some of the differences that show up. Let's take some time here to explore the different parts of artificial intelligence and Machine Learning so we can see how these are the same and how they are different.

What is artificial intelligence?

The first thing we are going to take a look at is artificial intelligence or AI. This is a term that was first brought about by a computer scientist named John McCarthy in the 1950s. AI was first described as a method that you would use for manufactured devices to learn how to copy the capabilities of humans concerning mental tasks.

However, the term has changed a bit in modern times, but you will find that the basic idea is the same. When you implement AI, you are enabling machines, such as computers, to operate and think just like the human brain can. This is a benefit that means that these AI devices are going to be more efficient at completing some tasks than the human brain.

At first glance, this may seem like AI is the same as Machine Learning, but they are not exactly the same. Some people who don't understand how these two terms work can think that they are the same, but the way that you use them in programming is going to make a big difference.

How is Machine Learning different?

Now that we have an idea of what artificial intelligence is all about, it is time to take a look at Machine Learning and how this is the same as artificial intelligence, and how this is different. When we look at Machine Learning, we are going to see that this is a bit newer than a few of the other options that come with Data Science as it is only about 20 years old. Even though it has been around for a few decades so far, it has been in the past few years that our technology and the machines that we have are finally able to catch up to this and Machine Learning is being used more.

Machine learning is unique because it is a part of Data Science that can focus just on having the program learn from the input, as well as the data that the user gives to it. This is useful because the algorithm will be able to take that information and make some good predictions. Let's look at an example of using a search engine. For this to work, you would just need to put in a term to a search query, and then the search engine would be able to look through the information that is there to see what matches up with that and returns some results.

The first few times that you do these search queries, it is likely that the results will have something of interest, but you may have to go down the page a bit to find the information that you want. But as you keep doing this, the computer will take that information and learn from it to provide you with choices that are better in the future. The first time, you may click on like the sixth result, but over time, you may click on the first or second result because the computer has learned what you find valuable.

With traditional programming, this is not something that your computer can do on its own. Each person is going to do searches differently, and there are millions of pages to sort through. Plus, each person who is doing their searches online will have their preferences for what they want to show up. Conventional programming is going to run into issues when you try to do this kind of task because there are just too many variables. Machine learning has the capabilities to make it happen though.

Of course, this is just one example of how you can use Machine Learning. In fact, Machine Learning can help you do some of these complex problems that you want the computer to solve. Sometimes, you can solve these issues with the human brain, but you will often find that Machine Learning is more efficient and faster than what the human brain can do.

Of course, it is possible to have someone manually go through and do this for you as well, but you can imagine that this would take too much time and be an enormous undertaking. There is too much information, they may have no idea where to even get started when it comes to sorting through it, the information can confuse them, and by the time they get through it all, too much time has passed and the information, as well as the predictions that come out of it, are no longer relevant to the company at all.

Machine learning changes the game because it can keep up. The algorithms that you can use with it can handle all of the work while getting the results back that you need, in almost real-time. This is one of the big reasons that businesses find that it is one of the best options to go with to help them make good and sound decisions, to help them predict the future, and it is a welcome addition to their business model.

Data Aggregation and Group Operations

Taking the time to categorize our set of data, and giving a function to each of the different groups that we have, whether it is transformation or aggregation, is often going to be a critical part of the workflow for data analysis. After we take the time to load, merge, and prepare a set of data, it is then time to compute some more information, such as the group statistics or the pivot tables. This is done to help with reporting or with visualizations of that data.

There are a few options that we can work with here to get this process done. But Pandas is one of the best because it provides us with a flexible interface. We can use this interface to slice, dice, and then summarize some of the sets of data we have more easily.

One reason that we see a lot of popularity for SQL and relational databases of all kinds is that we can use them to ease up the process which joins, filters, transforms, and aggregates the data that we have. However, some of the query languages, including SQL, that we want to use are going to be more constrained in the kinds of group operations that we can perform right with them.

As we are going to see with some of the expressiveness that happens with the Pandas library, and with Python, in general, we can perform a lot of more complex operations. This is done by simply utilizing any function that can accept an array from NumPy or an object from Pandas.

Each of the grouping keys that you want to work with can end up taking a variety of forms. And we can see that the keys don't have to all come in as the same type. Some of the forms that these grouping keys can come in for us to work on include:

1. An array or a list that is the same length as the axis that we want to group.

2. A value that is going to indicate the name of the column in a DataFrame.

3. A Series that is going to give the correspondence between the values of the axis that is being grouped here, and the group names you have.

4. A function that can then be invoked on the axis index, or on some of the individual labels in the index.

Note that the last three methods of this are going to be a type of shortcut that helps us to produce an array of values to be used when splitting up the object. This can seem a bit abstract right now, but don't let this bother you. It will all make more sense as we go through the steps and learn more about how all of this is meant to work. With this in mind, it is time to talk more about data aggregation and how we can make this work for our needs.

What Is Data Aggregation

Data aggregation is any kind of process in which information can be gathered and then expressed in the form of a summary, usually for analysis. One of the common purposes that come with aggregation is to help us get some more information about a particular topic or a group, based on a lot of variables like profession, income, and age.

The information about these groups is often going to be used to personalize a website, allowing them to choose what content and advertising that is likely to appeal to an individual who belongs to one or more groups where the data was originally collected from. Let's take a look at how this works.

We can work with a site that is responsible for selling music CDs. They could use the ideas of data aggregation to advertise specific types of CD's based on the age of the user, and the data aggregate that is collected for others in that age group. The OLAP, or Online Analytic Processing, is a simple option with data aggregation in which the market is going to use mechanisms for online reporting to help the business process through all of this information.

Data aggregation can be a lot of different things as well. For example, it could be more user-based than some of the other programs that we may have seen in the past. Personal data aggregation services are popular, and they will offer any user a single point for collection of their personal information from a host of other websites that we want to work with.

In these systems, the customer is going to work with a single master PIN, or personal identification number, which allows them the access they need to various accounts. this could include things like music clubs, book clubs, airlines, financial institutions, and so on. Performing this type of data aggregation can take some time and will be a more complex system to put in, but we will see that it comes under the title of screen scraping.

This is just one example of how we can work through the process of data aggregation. It is one of the best methods to help companies to gain the knowledge and the power that they need based on the users they have at the time. it often works well with Pandas, Python, and even databases because it can collect a lot of the information that is found in those, and then recommends options to our customers or our users, based on where they fit in with the rest of the information.

Yes, there are always going to be some outliers to the information, and times when the information is not going to apply to a person no matter where they fit in the database or how good the data aggregation algorithms are. But it will be able to increase the likelihood that you will reach the customers and the users you want, providing them with the information and the content that they need, based on their features and how they will react compared to other similar customers.

Practical Codes and Exercises to Use Python

Now that we have had some time to learn how to work with the Python code, it is time to take a look at some practical examples of working with this kind of coding language. We will do a few different Python exercises here so that you can have a little bit of fun, and get a better idea of how you would use the different topics that we have talked about in this guidebook to your benefit. There are a lot of neat programs that you can use when you write in Python, but the ones in this chapter will give you a good idea of how to write codes, and how to use the examples that we talked about in this guidebook in real coding. So let's get started!

Creating a Magic 8 Ball

The first project that we are going to take a look at here is how to create your own Magic 8 ball. This will work just like a regular magic 8 ball, but it will be on the computer. You can choose how many answers that you would like to have available to those who are using the program but we are going to focus on having eight responses show up for the user at a random order so they get something different each time.

Setting up this code is easier than you think. Take some time to study this code, and then write it out into the compiler. See how many of the different topics we discussed in this guidebook show up in this code as well. The code that you need to use to create a program that includes your own Magic 8 ball will include:

```
# Import the modules
```

```
import sys
import random
ans = True
while ans:
question = raw_input("Ask the magic 8 ball a question: (press enter to quit)")
answers = random.randint(1,8)
if question == ""
sys.exit()
elif answers ==1:
print("It is certain")
elif answers == 2:
print("Outlook good")
elif answers == 3:
print("You may rely on it")
elif answers == 4:
print("Ask again later")

elif answers == 5:
print("Concentrate and ask again")
elif answers == 6:
print("Reply hazy, try again.")
elif answers == 7:
print("My reply is no")
elif answers == 8:
print("My sources say no")
```

Remember in this program, we chose to go with eight options because it is a Magic 8 ball and that makes the most sense. But if you would like to add in some more options, or work on another program that is similar and has more options, then you would just need to keep adding in more of the elif statement to get it done. This is still a good example of how to use the elif statement that we talked about earlier and can give us some good practice on how to use it. You can also experiment a bit with the program to see how well it works and make any changes that you think are necessary to help you get the best results.

How to make a Hangman Game

The next project that we are going to take a look at is creating your own Hangman game. This is a great game to create because it has a lot of the different options that we have talked about throughout this guidebook and can be a great way to get some practice on the various topics that we have looked at. We are going to see things like a loop present, some comments, and more and this is a good way to work with some of the conditional statements that show up as well.

Now, you may be looking at this topic and thinking it is going to be hard to work with a Hangman game. It is going to have a lot of parts that go together as the person makes a guess and the program tries to figure out what is going on, whether the guesses are right, and how many chances the user gets to make these guesses. But using a lot of the different parts that we have already talked about in this guidebook can help us to write out this code without any problems. The code that you need to use to create your very own Hangman game in Python includes:

```
# importing the time module
importing time
#welcoming the user
Name = raw_input("What is your name?")
print("Hello, + name, "Time to play hangman!")
print("
```

```
"
#wait for 1 second
time.sleep(1)
print("Start guessing…")
time.sleep(.05)
#here we set the secret
word = "secret"
#creates a variable with an empty value
guesses = ' '
#determine the number of turns
turns = 10
#create a while loop
#check if the turns are more than zero
while turns > 0:
#make a counter that starts with zero
failed = 0
#for every character in secret_word
for car in word:
#see if the character is in the players guess
if char in guesses:

#print then out the character
print char,
else
# if not found, print a dash
print "_",

# and increase the failed counter with one
failed += 1
#if failed is equal to zero
#print You Won
if failed == 0:
print("You Won")
```

```
#exit the script
Break
print
# ask the user to guess a character
guess = raw_input("guess a character:")
#set the players guess to guesses
guesses += guess
# if the guess is not found in the secret word
if guess not in word:
#turns counter decreases with 1 (now 9)
turns -= 1
#print wrong
print("Wrong")
# how many turns are left
Print("You have," + turns, 'more guesses')
#if the turns are equal to zero
if turns == 0
#print "You Lose"
```

Okay, so yes, this is a longer piece of code, especially when it is compared to the Magic 8 Ball that we did above, but take a deep breath, and go through it all to see what you recognize is there. This isn't as bad as it looks, and much of it is comments to help us see what is going on at some of the different parts of the code. This makes it easier to use for our own needs and can ensure that we know what is going on in the different parts. There are probably a lot of other things that show up in this code that you can look over and recognize that we talked about earlier as well. This makes it easier for you to get the code done!

Making your own K-means algorithm

Now that we have had some time to look at a few fun games and examples that you can do with the help of the Python code, let's take a moment to look at some of the things that you can do with Machine Learning and artificial intelligence with your coding. We spent some time talking about how you can work with these and some of the different parts of the code, as well as how Python is going to work with the idea of Machine Learning. And now we are going to take that information and create one of our Machine Learning algorithms to work with as well.

Before we work on a code for this one, we need to take a look at what this k-means clustering means. This is a basic algorithm that works well with Machine Learning and is going to help you to gather up all of the data that you have in your system, the data that isn't labeled at the time, and then puts them all together in their little group of a cluster.

The idea of working with this kind of cluster is that the objects that fall within the same cluster, whether there are just two or more, are going to be related to each other in some manner or another, and they are not going to be that similar to the data points that fall into the other clusters. The similarity here is going to be the metric that you will want to use to show us the strength that is in the relationship between the two.

When you work on this particular algorithm, it is going to be able to form some of the clusters that you need of the data, based on how similar the values of data that you have. You will need to go through and give them a specific value for K, which will be how many clusters that you would like to use. It is best to have at least two, but the number of these clusters that you work with will depend on how much data you have and how many will fit in with the type of data that you are working with.

With this information in mind and a good background of what the K-means algorithm is going to be used for, it is time to explore a bit more about how to write your own codes and do an example that works with K-means. This helps us to practice a bit with Machine Learning and gives us a chance to practice some of our own new Python skills.

```python
import numpy as np
import matplotlib.pyplot as plt
def d(u, v):
    diff = u - v
    return diff.dot(diff)
def cost(X, R, M):
    cost = 0
    for k in xrange(len(M)):
        for n in xrange(len(X)):
            cost += R[n,k]*d(M[k], X[n])
    return cost
```

After this part, we are going to take the time to define your function so that it is able to run the k-means algorithm before plotting the result. This is going to end up with a scatterplot where the color will represent how much of the membership is inside of a particular cluster. We would do that with the following code.

```python
def plot_k_means(X, K, max_iter=20, beta=1.0):
    N, D = X.shape
    M = np.zeros((K, D))
    R = np.ones((N, K)) / K
    # initialize M to random
    for k in xrange(K):
```

```
        M[k] = X[np.random.choice(N)]
    grid_width = 5
    grid_height = max_iter / grid_width
    random_colors = np.random.random((K, 3))
    plt.figure()
    costs = np.zeros(max_iter)
    for i in xrange(max_iter):
        # moved the plot inside the for loop
        colors = R.dot(random_colors)
        plt.subplot(grid_width, grid_height, i+1)
        plt.scatter(X[:,0], X[:,1], c=colors)
        # step 1: determine assignments / responsibilities
        # is this inefficient?
        for k in xrange(K):
            for n in xrange(N):
                R[n,k] = np.exp(-beta*d(M[k], X[n])) / np.sum( np.exp(-beta*d(M[j], X[n])) for j in xrange(K) )
        # step 2: recalculate means
        for k in xrange(K):
            M[k] = R[:,k].dot(X) / R[:,k].sum()
        costs[i] = cost(X, R, M)
        if i > 0:
            if np.abs(costs[i] - costs[i-1]) < 10e-5:
                break
    plt.show()
```

Notice here that both the M and the R are going to be matrices. The R is going to become the matrix because it holds onto 2 indices, the k and the n. M is also a matrix because it is going to contain the K individual D-dimensional vectors. The beta variable is going to control how fuzzy or spread out the cluster memberships are and will be known as the hyperparameter. From here, we are going to create a main function that will create random clusters and then call up the functions that we have already defined above.

```
def main():
    # assume 3 means
    D = 2 # so we can visualize it more easily
    s = 4 # separation so we can control how far apart the means are
    mu1 = np.array([0, 0])
    mu2 = np.array([s, s])
    mu3 = np.array([0, s])
    N = 900 # number of samples
    X = np.zeros((N, D))
    X[:300, :] = np.random.randn(300, D) + mu1
    X[300:600, :] = np.random.randn(300, D) + mu2
    X[600:, :] = np.random.randn(300, D) + mu3
    # what does it look like without clustering?
    plt.scatter(X[:,0], X[:,1])
    plt.show()
    K = 3 # luckily, we already know this
    plot_k_means(X, K)
    # K = 5 # what happens if we choose a "bad" K?
    # plot_k_means(X, K, max_iter=30)
    # K = 5 # what happens if we change beta?
    # plot_k_means(X, K, max_iter=30, beta=0.3)
if __name__ == '__main__':
    main()
```

Yes, this process is going to take some time to write out here, and it is not always an easy process when it comes to working through the different parts that come with Machine Learning and how it can affect your code. But when you are done, you will be able to import some of the data that your company has been collecting, and then determine how this compares using the K-means algorithm as well.

Functions and Modules in Python

In Python programming, functions refer to any group of related statements that perform a given activity. Functions are used in breaking down programs into smaller and modular bits. In that sense, functions are the key factors that make programs easier to manage and organize as they grow bigger over time. Functions are also helpful in avoiding repetition during coding and make codes reusable.

The Syntax of Functions

The syntax of functions refers to the rules which govern the combination of characters that make up a function. These syntaxes include the following:

- The keyword "def" highlights the beginning of every function header.
- A function named is to identify it distinctly. The rules of making functions are the same as the rules which apply for writing identifiers in Python.
- Parameters or arguments via which values are passed onto a function are optional in Python.
- A colon sign (:) is used to highlight the end of every function header.
- The optional documentation string known as "docstring" is used to define the purpose of the function.
- The body of a function is comprised of one or more valid statements in Python. The statements must all have a similar

indentation level, (typically four spaces).
- An optional return statement is included for returning a value from a function.

Below is a representation of the essential components of a function as described in the syntax.

```
def function_name(parameters):
'''docstring'''
statement(s)
```

How Functions are Called in Python

Once a function has been defined in Python, it is capable of being called from another function, a program, or the Python prompt even. Calling a function is done by entering a function name with a proper parameter.

Docstring

The docstring is the first string that comes after the function header. The docstring is short for documentation string and is used in explaining what a function does briefly. Although it is an optional part of a function, the documentation process is a good practice in programming. So, unless you have got an excellent memory that can recall what you had for breakfast on your first birthday, you should document your code at all times. In the example shown below, the docstring is used directly beneath the function header.

```
>>> greet("Amos")
```

```
Hello, Amos. Good morning!
```

Triple quotation marks are typically used when writing docstrings so they can extend to several lines. Such a string is inputted as the __doc__ attribute of the function. Take the example below.

You can run the following lines of code in a Python shell and see what it outputs:

```
>>> print(greet.__doc__)
This function greets to the person passed into the name parameter
```

The return statement

The purpose of the return statement is to go back to the location from which it was called after exiting a function.

Syntax of return

This statement can hold expressions that have been evaluated and have their values returned. A function will return the Noneobject if the statement is without an expression, or its return statement is itself absent in the function.

For instance:

```
>>> print(greet('Amos'))
Hello, Amos. Good morning!
None
```

In this case, the returned value is None.

Interaction with Databases

Data management is not a scientific discipline per se. However, increasingly, it permeates the activities of basic scientific work. The increasing volume of data and increasing complexity has long exceeded manageability through simple spreadsheets.

Currently, the need to store quantitative, qualitative data and media of different formats (images, videos, sounds) is very common in an integrated platform from which they can be easily accessed for analysis, visualization or simply consultation.

The Python language has simple solutions to solve this need at its most different levels of sophistication. Following the Python included batteries, its standard library introduces us to the Pickle and cPickle module and, starting with Version 2.5, the SQLite3 relational database.

The Pickle Module

The pickle module and its fastest cPickle cousin implement algorithms that allow you to store Python-implemented objects in a file.

Example of using the pickle module

```
import pickle
class hi:
  def say_hi (self):
    print " hi "
a= hi()
f= open ('pic test','w')
```

```
pickle.dump(a, f)
f.close()
f= open ('pic test','r')
b=pickle.load (f)
b.say_hi()
hi
```

As we see in the example of using the pickle module, with the pickle module we can store objects in a file, and retrieve it without problems for later use. However, an important feature of this module is not evident in example 8.1. When an object is stored using the pickle module, neither the class code nor its data are included, only the instance data.

```
class hi:
   def say_hi (self, name=' alex'):
     print'hi %s !'%name

f= open ('pictest','r')
b=pickle.load (f)
b.say_hi()
hi alex !
```

This way we can modify the class, and the stored instance will recognize the new code as it is restored from the file, as we can see above. This feature means that pickles do not become obsolete when the code they are based on is updated (of course this is only for modifications that do not remove attributes already included in the pickles).

The pickle module is not built for data storage, simply, but for complex computational objects that may contain data themselves. Despite this versatility, it is because it consists of a readable storage structure only by the pickle module itself in a Python program.

The SQLite3 Module

This module becomes part of the standard Python library from Version 2.5. Therefore, it becomes an excellent alternative for users who require the functionality of an SQL1-compliant relational database.

SQLite was born from a C library that had an extremely lightweight database and no concept client-server. In SQLite, the database is a file handled through the SQLite library.

To use SQLite in a Python program, we need to import the SQLite3 module.

```
import sqlite3
```

The next step is the creation of a connection object, through which we can execute SQL commands.

```
c= sqlite 3.connect (' /tmp/ example')
```

We now have an empty database consisting of the example file located in the / tmp directory. SQLite also allows the creation of RAM databases. To do this, simply replace the file name with the string: memory. To insert data into this database, we must first create a table.

```
c.execute (''' create table  specimens (name text,
real height, real weight)''')
< sqlite 3.Cursor object at 0 x83fed10 >
```

Note that SQL commands are sent as strings through the Connection object, execute method. The *create table* command creates a table; it must necessarily be followed by the table name and a list of typed variables (in parentheses), corresponding to the variables contained in this table. This command creates only the table structure. Each specified variable will correspond to one column of the table. Each subsequent entry will form a table row.

```
c.execute ("' insert into  specimens values (' tom', 1 2.5, 2.3)'")
```

The insert command is another useful SQL command for inserting records into a table.

Although SQL commands are sent as strings over the connection, it is not recommended, for security reasons, to use the string formatting methods ('... values (% s,% s)'% (1,2)) of Python Instead, do the following:

```
t= (' tom',)
c.execute ('select from  specimens where name=?', t)
c.fetch all()
[(' tom', 1 2.5, 2.2 9 9 9 9 9 9 9 9 9 9 9 9 9 9 8)]
```

In the example above we use the fetchall method to retrieve the result of the operation. If we wanted to get a single record, we would use fetchone.

Below is how to insert more than one record from existing data structures. In this case, it is a matter of repeating the operation described in the previous example, with a sequence of tubes representing the sequence of records to be inserted.

```
t= ((' j e r r y', 5.1, 0.2), (' butch', 4 2.4, 1 0.3))
for i in t:
   c.execute (' insert into  specimens value s (?, ?, ?)', i)
```

The cursor object can also be used as an iterator to get the result of a query.

```
c.execute (' selectfrom specimens by weight')
for reg in c:
```

```
    print reg
(' jerry', 5.1, 0.2)
(' tom', 1 2.5, 2.2 9 9 9 9 9 9 9 9 9 9 9 9 9 9 8)
(' butch', 4 2.4, 1 0.3)
```

The SQLite module is really versatile and useful, but it requires the user to know at least the rudiments of the SQL language. The following solution seeks to solve this problem in a more Pythonic way.

The SQLObject Package

The SQLObject2 package extends the solutions presented so far in two ways: it offers an object-oriented interface to relational databases, and also allows us to interact with multiple databases without having to change our code.

To exemplify sqlobject, we will continue to use SQLite because of its practicality.

Building a Digital Spider

In this example, we will have the opportunity to build a digital spider that will gather information from the web (Wikipedia3) and store it in an SQLite bank via sqlobject.

For this example, we will need some tools that go beyond the database. Let's explore the ability of the standard Python library to interact with the internet, and let's use an external package to decode the pages obtained.

The BeautifulSoup4package is a webpage breaker. One of the most common problems when dealing with Html pages is that many of them have minor design flaws that our browsers ignore, but can hinder further scrutiny.

Hence the value of BeautifulSoup: it is capable of handling faulty pages, returning a data structure with methods that allow quick and simple extraction of the desired information. Also, if the page was created using another encoding, BeautifulSoup, returns all Unicode content automatically without user intervention.

From the standard library, we will use the sys, os, urllib, urllib2 and re modules. The usefulness of each character becomes clear as we move forward in the example.

The first step is to specify the database. SQLObject allows us to choose from MySQL, PostgreSQL, SQLite, Firebird, MAXDB, Sybase, MSSQL, or ADODBAPI. However, as we have already explained, we will restrict ourselves to using the SQLite bank.

Specifying the Database

```
johnsmith= os.path.expanduser (' ~ /. johnsmith' )
if not os.path.exists (at the dir):
os.mkdir (at the dir)
sqlhub.process Connection = connectionForURI ('
sqlite://'+johnsmithr +'/knowdb')
```

In specifying the database, we create the directory (os.mkdir) where the database will reside (if necessary) and we will natively connect to the database. We use os.path.exists to check if the directory exists. Since we want the directory in the user's folder, and we have no way of knowing beforehand what this directory is, we use os.path.expanduser to replace / home/user as it would normally on the Unix console.

On line 11 of Specifying the database, we see the command that creates the connection to be used by all objects created in this module.

Next, we specify our database table as a class, in which its attributes are the table columns.

Specifying the database ideatable

```
class Idea (SQLObject): name= UnicodeCol() nlinks= IntCol()
links= Pickle Col() address = StringCol
```

The class that represents our table is inherited from the SQLObject class. In this class, each attribute (table column) must be assigned an object that gives the type of data to be stored. In this example, we see four distinct types, but there are several others. UnicodeCol represents texts encoded as Unicode, i.e. it can contain characters from any language. IntCol is integer numbers. PickleCol is an exciting type as it allows you to store any type of Python object.

The most interesting thing about this type of column is that it does not require the user to invoke the pickle module to store or read this type of variable. Variables are automatically converted/converted according to the operation. Finally, we have StringCol which is a simpler version of UnicodeCol, accepting only ASCII character strings. In SQL it is common to have terms that specify different types according to the length of the text you want to store in a variable. In sqlobject, there is no limit to the size of the text that can be stored in either StringCol or UnicodeCol.

The functionality of our spider has been divided into two classes: Crawler, which is the creeper itself, and the UrlFac class that builds URLs from the word you want in Wikipedia.

Each page is pulled by the urllib2 module. The urlencode function of the urllib module makes it easy to add data to our request so as not to show that it comes from a digital spider. Without this disguise, Wikipedia refuses the connection.

The pages are then parsed by the VerResp method, where BeautifulSoup has a chance to do its work. Using the SoupStrainer function, we can find the rest of the document, which doesn't interest us, by analyzing only the links (tags 'a') whose destination is URLs beginning with the string/wiki/. All Wikipedia articles start this way. Thus, we avoid chasing external links. From the soup produced we extract only the URLs, i.e. what comes after "href =".

Data Mining Techniques in Data Science

The basics of Math and Statistics help a data scientist to build, analyze, and create some complex analytics. To draw accurate insights about the data, data scientists are required to interact with the business side. Business Acumen is a necessity when it comes to analyzing data to help out the business. The results must also be in line with the expectations of the businesses. Therefore, the ability to verbally and visually communicate advanced results and observations to the business and help them easily understand. Data Mining is such a strategy used in Data Science that describes the process where raw data are structured in such a way where one can recognize patterns in the data via mathematical and computational algorithms. Let us an overview of five major data Mining Techniques that every data scientist must be aware of.

Mapreduce Technique

Data Mining applications manage vast amounts of data constantly. You must opt for a new software stack to tackle such applications. Stack software has its file system stored that is called a distributed file system. This file system is used for retrieving parallelism from a computing cluster or clusters. This distributed file system replicates data to enforce security against media failures. Other than this stack file system, there is a higher-level programming system developed to ease the process viz. Mapreduce. Mapreduce is a form of computed implemented in various systems, including Hadoop and Google. Mapreduce implementation is a data mining technique used to tackle large-scale computations. It is easy to implement, i.e.; you have to type only three functions viz. Map and Reduce. The system will automatically control parallel execution and task collaboration.

Distance Measures

The main limitation of data Mining is that it is unable to track similar data/items. Consider an example where you have to track duplicate websites or web content while browsing various websites. Another example can be discovering similar images from a large database. To handle such problems, the Distance Measure technique is made available to you. Distance Measure helps to search for the nearest neighbors in a higher-dimensional space. It is very crucial to define what similarity is. Jaccard Similarity can be one of the examples. The methods used to identify similarity and define the Distance Measure Technique

- Shingling
- Min-Hashing

- Locality Sensitive Hashing

- A K-Shingle

- Locality-Sensitive Hashing

Link Analysis

Link Analysis is performed when you can scan the spam vulnerabilities. Earlier, most of the traditional search engines failed to scan the spam vulnerabilities. However, as technology got its wings, Google was able to Introduce some techniques to overcome this problem.

Pagerank

Pagerank techniques use the method of simulation. It monitors every page you are surfing to scan spam vulnerability. This whole process works iteratively, meaning pages that have a higher number of users are ranked better than pages without users visiting.

The Content

The content on every page is determined by some specific phrases used in a page to link with external pages. It is a piece of cake for spammers to modify the internal page where they are administrators, but it becomes difficult for them to modify the external pages. Every page is allocated a real number via a function. The page with a higher rank becomes more important than the page that does not have a considerable page rank. There are no algorithms set for assigning ranks to pages. But for highly confidential or connected Web Graphics, they have a transition matrix based ranking. This principle is used for calculating the rank of a page.

Data Streaming

At times, it is difficult to know datasets in advance; also, the data appears in the form of a stream and gets processed before it disappears. The speed of arrival of the data is so fast that it is difficult to store them in the active storage. Here, data streaming comes into the picture. In the dataStream management system, an unlimited number of streams can be stored in a system. Each data stream produces elements at its own time. Elements have the same rate and time in a particular stream cycle. Such streams are archived into the store. By doing this, it is somewhat difficult to reply to queries already stored in the archival. But such situations are handled by specific retrieval methods. There is a working store as well as an active store that stores the summaries to reply to specific queries. There are certain data Streaming problems viz.

Sampling data in a Stream

You will select attributes to create some samples of the streams. To determine whether all the sample elements belong to the same key sample, you will have to rotate the hashing key of the incoming stream element.

Filtering Streams

To select specific tuples to fit a particular criterion, there is a separate process where the accepted tuples are carried forward, whereas others are terminated and eliminated. There is a modern technique known as Bloon Filtering that will allow you to filter out the foreign elements. The later process is that the selected elements are hashed and collected into buckets to form bits. Bits have a binary working, i.e., 0 and 1. Such bits are set to 1. After this, the elements are set to be tested.

Count Specific Elements in a Stream

If you require to count the unique elements that exist in a universal set, you might have to count each element from the initial step. Flajolet-Martin is a method that often hashes elements to integers, described as binary numbers. By using hash functions and integrating them may result in a reliable estimate.

Frequent Item – Set Analysis

In Frequent Item Set Analysis, we will check the market-basket model and the relationship between them. Every basket contains a set of items, whereas the market will have the data information. The total number of items is always higher than the number of items in the basket. This implies the number of items in the basket can fit in the memory. Baskets are the original and genuine files in the overall distributed system. Each basket is a set of items type. To conclude on the market-basket technique, the characterization of the data depends on this technique to discover frequent itemset. Such sets of items are responsible for revealing most of the baskets. There are many use cases available over the Internet for this technique. This technique was applied previously in some big malls, supermarkets, and chain stores. To illustrate this case, such stores keep track of each of the basket that customer brings to the checkout counter. Here, the items represent the products sold by the store, whereas baskets are a set of items found in a single basket.

Data in the Cloud

Data science is a mixture of many concepts. To become a data scientist, it is important to have some programming skills. Even though you might not know all the programming concepts related to infrastructure, but having basic skills in computer science concepts is a must. You must install the two most common and most used programming languages i.e., R and Python, on your computer. With the ever-expanding advanced analytics, Data Science continues to spread its wings in different directions. This requires collaborative solutions like predictive analysis and recommendation systems. Collaboration solutions include research and notebook tools integrated with code source control. Data science is also related to the cloud. The information is also stored in the cloud. So, this lesson will enlighten you with some facts about the "data in the Cloud." So let us understand what cloud means and how the data are stored and how it works.

What is the Cloud?

Cloud can be described as a global server network, each having different unique functions. Understanding networks is required to study the cloud. Networks can be simple or complex clusters of information or data.

Network

As specified earlier, networks can have a simple or small group of computers connected or large groups of computers connected. The largest network can be the Internet. The small groups can be home local networks like Wi-Fi, and Local Area Network that is limited to certain computers or locality. There are shared networks such as media, web pages, app servers, data storage, and printers, and scanners. Networks have nodes, where a computer is referred to as a node. The communication between these computers is established by using protocols. Protocols are the intermediary rules set for a computer. Protocols like HTTP, TCP, and IP are used on a large scale. All the information is stored in the computer, but it becomes difficult to search for information on the computer every time. Such information is usually stored in a data Centre. Data Centre is designed in such a way that it is equipped with support security and protection for the data. Since the cost of computers and storage has decreased substantially, multiple organizations opt to make use of multiple computers that work together that one wants to scale. This differs from other scaling solutions like buying other computing devices. The intent behind this is to keep the work going continuously even if a computer fails; the other will continue the operation. There is a need to scale some cloud applications, as well. Having a broad look at some computing applications like YouTube, Netflix, and Facebook that requires some scaling. We rarely experience such applications failing, as they have set up their systems on the cloud. There is a network cluster in the cloud, where many computers are connected to the same networks and accomplish similar tasks. You can call it as a single source of information or a single computer that manages everything to improve performance, scalability, and availability.

Data Science in the Cloud

The whole process of Data Science takes place in the local machine, i.e., a computer or laptop provided to the data scientist. The computer or laptop has inbuilt programming languages and a few more prerequisites installed. This can include common programming languages and some algorithms. The data scientist later has to install relevant software and development packages as per his/her project. Development packages can be installed using managers such as Anaconda or similar managers. You can opt for installing them manually too. Once you install and enter into the development environment, then your first step, i.e., the workflow starts where your companion is only data. It is not mandatory to carry out the task related to Data Science or Big data on different development machines. Check out the reasons behind this:

1. The processing time required to carry out tasks on the development environment fails due to processing power failure.
2. Presence of large data sets that cannot be contained in the development environment's system memory.
3. Deliverables must be arrayed into a production environment and incorporated as a component in a large application.
4. It is advised to use a machine that is fast and powerful.

Data scientist explores many options when they face such issues; they make use of on-premise machines or virtual machines that run on the cloud. Using virtual machines and auto-scaling clusters has various benefits, such as they can span up and discard it anytime in case it is required. Virtual machines are customized in a way that will fulfill one's computing power and storage needs. Deployment of the information in a production environment to push it in a large data pipeline may have certain challenges. These challenges are to be understood and analyzed by the data scientist. This can be understood by having a gist of software architectures and quality attributes.

Software Architecture and Quality Attributes

A cloud-based software system is developed by Software Architects. Such systems may be product or service that depends on the computing system. If you are building software, the main task includes the selection of the right programming language that is to be programmed. The purpose of the system can be questioned; hence, it needs to be considered. Developing and working with software architecture must be done by a highly skilled person. Most of the organizations have started implementing effective and reliable cloud environment using cloud computing. These cloud environments are deployed over to various servers, storage, and networking resources. This is used in abundance due to its less cost and high ROI.

The main benefit to data scientists or their teams is that they are using the big space in the cloud to explore more data and create important use cases. You can release a feature and have it tested the next second and check whether it adds value, or it is not useful to carry forward. All this immediate action is possible due to cloud computing.

Sharing Big Data in the Cloud

The role of Big Data is also vital while dealing with the cloud as it makes it easier to track and analyze insights. Once this is established, big data creates great value for users.

The traditional way was to process wired data. It became difficult for the team to share their information with this technique. The usual problems included transferring large amounts of data and collaboration of the same. This is where cloud computing started sowing its seed in the competitive world. All these problems were eliminated due to cloud computing, and gradually, teams were able to work together from different locations and overseas as well. Therefore, cloud computing is very vital in both Data Science as well as Big data. Most of the organizations make use of the cloud. To illustrate, a few companies that use the cloud are Swiggy, Uber, Airbnb, etc. They use cloud computing for sharing information and data.

Cloud and Big Data Governance

Working with the cloud is a great experience as it reduces resource cost, time, and manual efforts. But the question arises that how organizations deal with security, compliance, governance? Regulation of the same is a challenge for most companies. Not limited to Big data problems, but working with the cloud also has its issues related to privacy and security. Hence, it is required to develop a strong governance policy in your cloud solutions. To ensure that your cloud solutions are reliable, robust, and governable, you must keep it as an open architecture.

Need for Data Cloud Tools to Deliver High Value of Data

Demand for a data scientist in this era is increasing rapidly. They are responsible for helping big and small organizations to develop useful information from the data or data set that is provided. Large organizations carry massive data that needs to analyze continuously. As per recent reports, almost 80% of the unstructured data received by the organizations are in the form of social media, emails, i.e., Outlook, Gmail, etc., videos, images, etc. With the rapid growth of cloud computing, data scientists deal with various new workloads that come from IoT, AI, Blockchain, Analytics, etc. Pipeline. Working with all these new workloads requires a stable, efficient, and centralized platform across all teams. With all this, there is a need for managing and recording new data as well as legacy documents. Once a data scientist is given a task, and he/she has the dataset to work on, he/she must possess the right skills to analyze the ever-increasing volumes through cloud technologies. They need to convert the data into useful insights that would be responsible for uplifting the business. The data scientist has to build an algorithm and code the program. They mostly utilize 80% of their time to gathering information, creating and modifying data, cleaning if required, and organizing data. Rest 20% is utilized for analyzing the data with effective programming. This calls for the requirement of having specific cloud tools to help the data scientist to reduce their time searching for appropriate information. Organizations should make available new cloud services and cloud tools to their respective data scientists so that they can organize massive data quickly. Therefore, cloud tools are very important for a data scientist to analyze large amounts of data at a shorter period. It will save the company's time and help build strong and robust data Models.

Conclusion

Thank You for making it through to the end!

The next step is to get started by seeing how Data Science is going to be able to work for your business. You will find that there are a lot of different ways that you can use the large amount of info that you have access to, and all of the data that you have been able to collect over time. Collecting the data is just the first step to the process. We also need to make sure that we can gain all of the insights and predictions that come out of that information, and this is where the process of Data Science is going to come into play.

This guidebook has taken some time to explore what Data Science is all about, and how it can help benefit your company in so many ways. We looked at some of the tasks that Data Science can help out with, what Data Science is and how to work with the life cycle of data, the future of data, and so much more. This helps us to see some of the parts that come to data analysis, and even how beneficial gathering and using all of that information can be to grow your business.

But this is not the only step that we can work with. We also need to take this a bit further and not just collect the data, but also be able to analyze that data and see what information it holds. This is a part of the Data Science life cycle, but it deserves some special attention because, without it, the data would just sit there without being used.

In this guidebook, we worked with the Python coding language and how this was able to help us to work through all of that data, collecting models and more, so we could learn something useful and make predictions about the data as well. This guidebook spent some time introducing Python and how it works and then moved on to some of the best libraries that you can use to not only write codes in Python but to use Python to work on the different models for analyzing the data you have.

Data science is a great thing to add to your business, and it can help you to make sure customer satisfaction is high, that waste is low, that you can make more money and can even help with predictions in the future, such as what products you should develop and put out on the market. But learning all of this is not something that just happens on its own. Working with Data Science, and adding in some Python language and the different libraries that are included with it can make the difference. When you are ready to work with Python Data Science to improve many different aspects of your own business and to beat out the competition, make sure to check out this guidebook to help you get started with it right away.

Printed in Great Britain
by Amazon